Poems and Pictures for Sharing

By

Swansea & District Writers' Circle

Copyright © 2024 by SDWC

All rights reserved. No part of this publication may be reproduced, stored or transmitted in any form or by any means, electronic, mechanical, photocopying, recording, scanning, or otherwise without written permission from the publisher. It is illegal to copy this book, post it to a website, or distribute it by any other means without permission.

First edition

The Story Book 7
The Open Door 11
She was Long and Yellow 13
Boundary Wall 17
Jellyfish 19
The Duck 21
Mother Knows Best 23
The Cat 27
The Fireworks of Spring 31
Chivalry 35
Forty-Eight 39
Miss Jennifer Pickles 41
Changing Seasons 45
Manic Panic 47
Sometimes I'm wise 49
Monkey Business 51
Choices 55
Sunset with Cows 57
Water Mill at Dunster Castle, Somerset 59
The Chosen One 61
Apple Blossom 63
Snowdrop 65
Sea Feverish 67

Goodbye, Arkwright…………………………………….71

James Bond……………………………………………..79

Mirror………………………………………………… 81

Light Breaks………………………………………….. 83

List of Resolutions……………………………………85

Throw It!.. 89

The New Sweep (Changing the idiom)…………… 91

Arthur Bell……………………………………………..93

Slinky Rat……………………………………………...95

The Unemployed Wildfowling Dog…………..………99

Acknowledgements………………………………… 107

Foreword

The poems in this book have all been written by the talented writers who are members of Swansea and District Writers' Circle (SDWC). The illustrations have been provided either by Circle members or with the aid of AI art (Nightcafe and Canva)

SDWC is all about promoting the art of writing in all its aspects.

Set up in 1954, we're still going strong and enjoy a loyal membership. We love to welcome new members, so if you have an interest in writing come and join us. We'd be happy to see you.

Preface

This book has been designed to be a fun and entertaining read. The poems are of the accessible variety - straightforward and relatable. They will take you through a range of feelings, and the pictures have been chosen to enhance the text. It is written in large text so that you can enjoy it in company as a shared reading experience. For this same reason, it is only available in hardback. It is much easier to hold a book open at arm's length if the covers are solid.

Reading aloud to someone can be very relaxing. It creates a special space for creative engagement and meaningful connections. We all enjoy watching the TV in company, but reading together is far more interactive and sociable.

The Story Book

By Paula Montez

We scan the shelf of books,

"Where shall we go today?

The chapters are all beckoning,

The bookmark charts the way.

Let's be fugitives of time

In the land of Never Never!"

We open up the cover

And our journey starts together.

From those precious pages,

The pixies skip and leap,

The coral bells start ringing,

Waking fairies from their sleep.

We tail them through the forest

'Til we're flying wing to wing,

They gather in a circle,

And we join them as they sing.

The story lifts us up

In the magic that it weaves.

On imagination's whim

We are wafting through the leaves.

The pages flutter forward,

Take us with them in their dance,

Enchanted forest raptures

Embrace us in a trance

Sparkling through the treetops,

Stars in symphony,

Our emotions intertwined

As we read in harmony.

Until it soothes to lullaby,

The Sandman walks abroad.

The pages softly settle,

And the book is safely stored.

The Open Door

By Paula Montez

The door is open, but only ajar,
Shall I go in or just call from afar?

The door is open, or is it half shut?
Shall I go in or shall I stay put?

The door is open, I can see through a crack.
Shall I go in or shall I hang back?

The door is open, I can see a white cat.
It purrs, it's friendly, ok that's that.

The door is open, I walk on through..
Uh oh,
"Hello Mr. Bond, we've been expecting you."

She was Long and Yellow

By Joan Darbyshire

She was long and yellow with fetching black stripes

And lived on a plant that was yellow and green.

She spent summer days eating and eating

And she grew and grew 'til the leaves were all gone.

When summer was over she fell to the soil

And created around her a shiny, brown shell.

All through the winter her body kept changing

Growing fatter with wings and antennae and legs.

As the weather grew warmer she wriggled upwards

'Til she reached the warmth of the springtime sun.

At the base of a plant, newly yellow and green,

She burst her shell and crawled up the stem.

A few hours later she spread her wings,

They had fetching patterns of red and black.

In her new beginning she flew round the plants,

With others just like her, for nectar and mates.

Laying her eggs on the plants green and yellow

Her purpose in life had now been completed.

So, if you think that your old life is ending

Its changes could be a new beginning.

Boundary Wall

By Mike Everley

Lines of syllabic stones in khaki brown
and grey. Cut, shaped and formed into the wall
that surrounds this park where children play ball.
A home to dog walkers and rough sleepers
where the homeless lay down their heads to rest.
Here nature is tamed and trimmed of excess.
But, in nooks away from the keeper's glance
wildness waits and grows ready for its chance.

Jellyfish

By Paula Montez

What if Jellyfish weren't transparent,

But rainbows floating wild,

Would their stings be less apparent?

Would we greet them with the tide?

The Duck

By Paula Montez

(A poem based on the song 'Lovely Day' by Bill Withers)

I wake up in the morning light,

The sunlight hits my….feathers.

Suddenly I'm all alight,

What happens next…Bill Withers?

Mother Knows Best

By Brian Vincent

It's don't do this and don't do that.

It's cold outside do wear a hat.

Fatty foods spoil a smooth complexion.

Don't pick that spot you'll cause infection.

Don't bite your nails, don't pick your nose;

And must you wear those scruffy clothes.

Your hair looks like a cuckoo's nest;

I like to see you smartly dressed.

Remember dear, your mother knows best.

When eating soup try not to slurp;

and please say pardon when you burp.

Must you swear like a dockyard porter;

I'll wash your mouth with soap and water.

Eat up, I want a nice clean plate.

Make sure you don't come in too late.

A growing boy needs lots of rest

And when you're tired you know you're stressed.

Remember dear, your mother knows best.

Tuck in that tum, you're overweight;

pull shoulders back, and stand up straight!

Mobile away now when you're eating;

don't rock that chair you'll break the seating.

Don't drag your feet so, when you walk,

and speak more clearly when you talk.

Do wrap up warm and wear a vest,

you know the cold goes to your chest.

Remember dear, your mother knows best.

Pleeeeeease. Mother dear, stop nagging me.

I'm married with three children and I'm pushing forty-three.

The Cat

By Fiona Riley

I'm spending my days wishing the cat would end hers

I know it sounds bad, but I've been waiting for years.

She's not horrid or scheming or filled up with spite,

And her face is just gorgeous with blue eyes so bright.

Her nature is gentle, her mew a sweet song

So why, you may ask, do I desire her gone?

To be perfectly frank I wish her no harm,

I like that she's happy, relaxed and so calm

But the crux of the matter, as I'll try to explain,

Is her scratching and moulting, it's just such a pain.

She's exiled to the kitchen because of her claws

For she scratches our sofa without conscience or pause.

If only she'd stop she'd have reign of the house

And then maybe no longer would I have to grouse.

Every movement she makes, sheds another few hairs,

My Hoover is blocked and my husband despairs.

The moulting's a problem with which to contend,

It's got to be sorted; I'm at my wits end.

But as I gaze down on this cute cat of mine

I know that our parting is way down the line.

She's loved by us all and is well fed and tended,

Maybe that's what's keeping her lifetime extended!

I'll never get rid of my soft silky friend,

When all's said and done, she's here to the end.

The Fireworks of Spring

By Paula Montez

Daring Daffodils bursting forth
Buttercup stars sprinkle the earth.
The wind whips fizzing branches of may,
Its blossoms in frenzy flutter away.
Dandelions like Catherine wheels.
Daisies glisten at their heels.
A bush in flaming orange regalia
A blazing bonfire, the scorching azalea.
Laburnum's dazzling golden cascade
And lupins leaping up in parade.
Pink petals of the thriving thrift
Splay and twinkle on the cliff.
And on the verges, either side,
Angelica is sparking wide.

The ever-dainty narcissus

Like smatterings of fairy dust.

Foxglove rockets reach up high

Chestnut shoots up to the sky.

Alliums sway in perfect spheres.

And rattle shakes its sparkling spear.

Celandines in gold array

Intersperse this bold display.

A Spectrum of colour, backdrop of green

Emerging from winter's bleakest scene

In Fresh, vivacious, vibrant zing -

These are the living fireworks of spring

Silent except for the whispering leaves

And bustling buzz of the bumble bees.

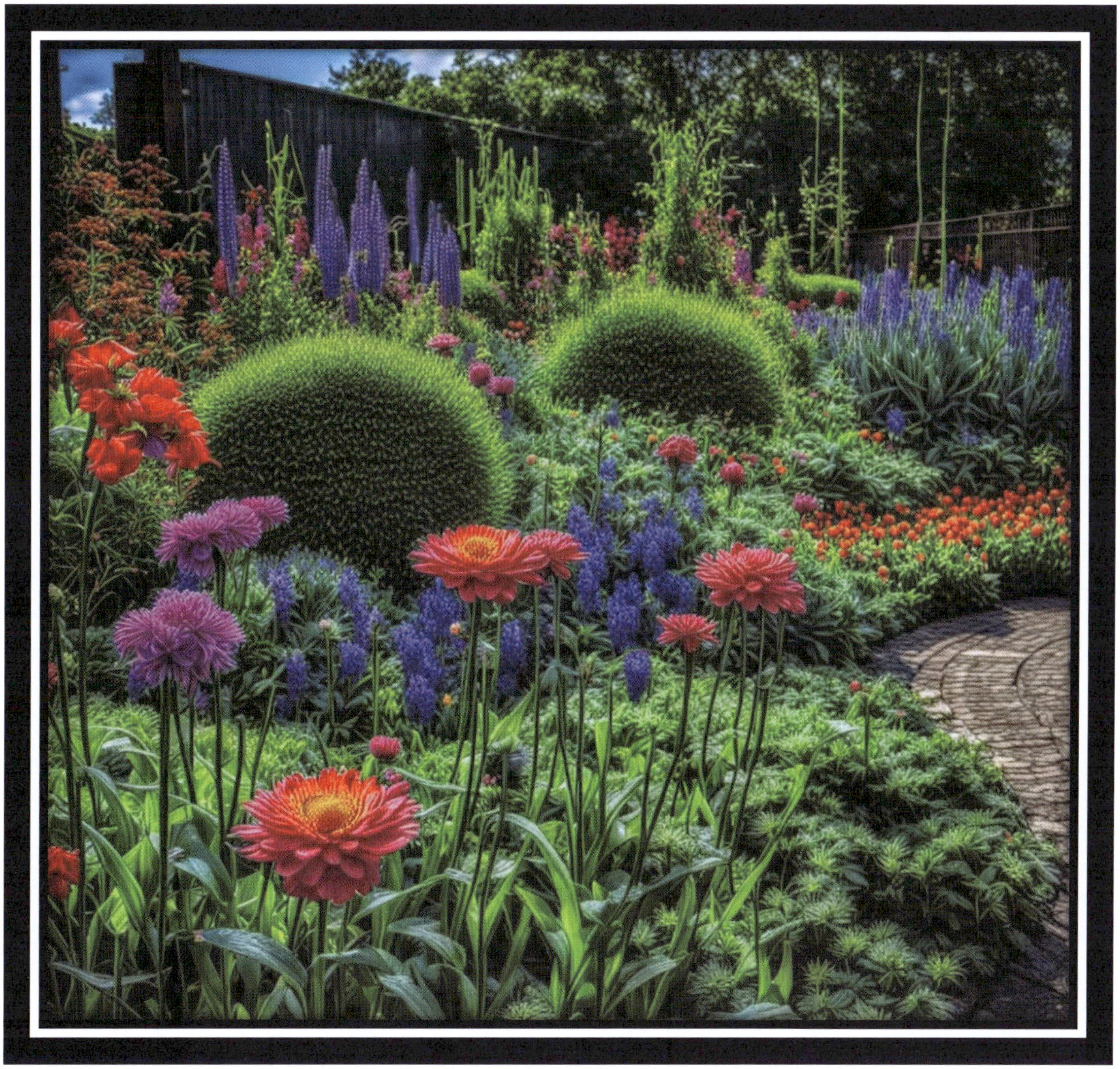

Chivalry

By Ann Marie Thomas

In days of old

the knights were bold -

or that's the way the rhyme goes.

But not today,

all gone away.

I wonder where the time goes?

They tell us tales

of holy grails

and chivalry and honour.

Today I'll bet

a girl will get

scorn only heaped upon her.

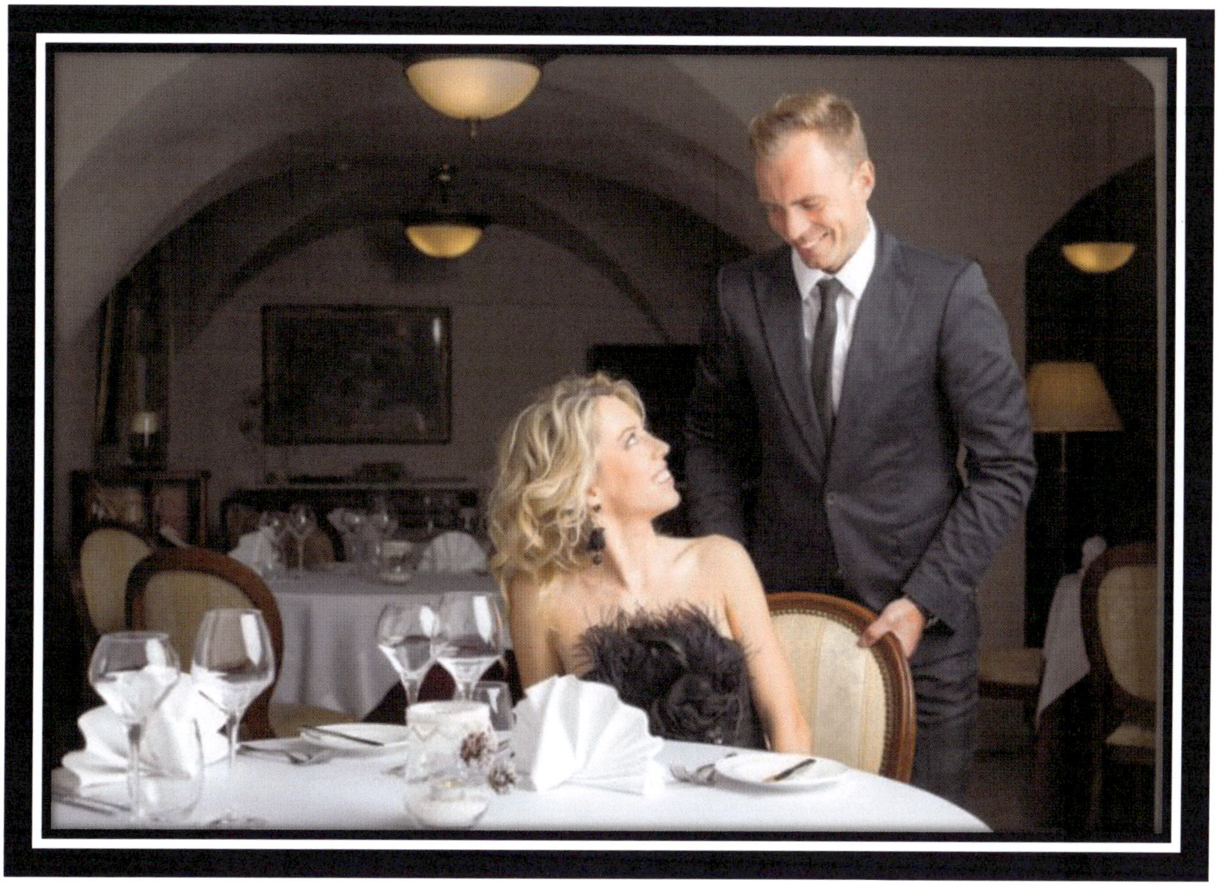

A maiden fair

who's in despair

is told to sort herself out.

This women's lib

has made men glib -

good manners have been thrown out.

Oh come again

when men were men

and women could be tender.

So be, my lad,

Sir Galahad,

and gladly I'll surrender.

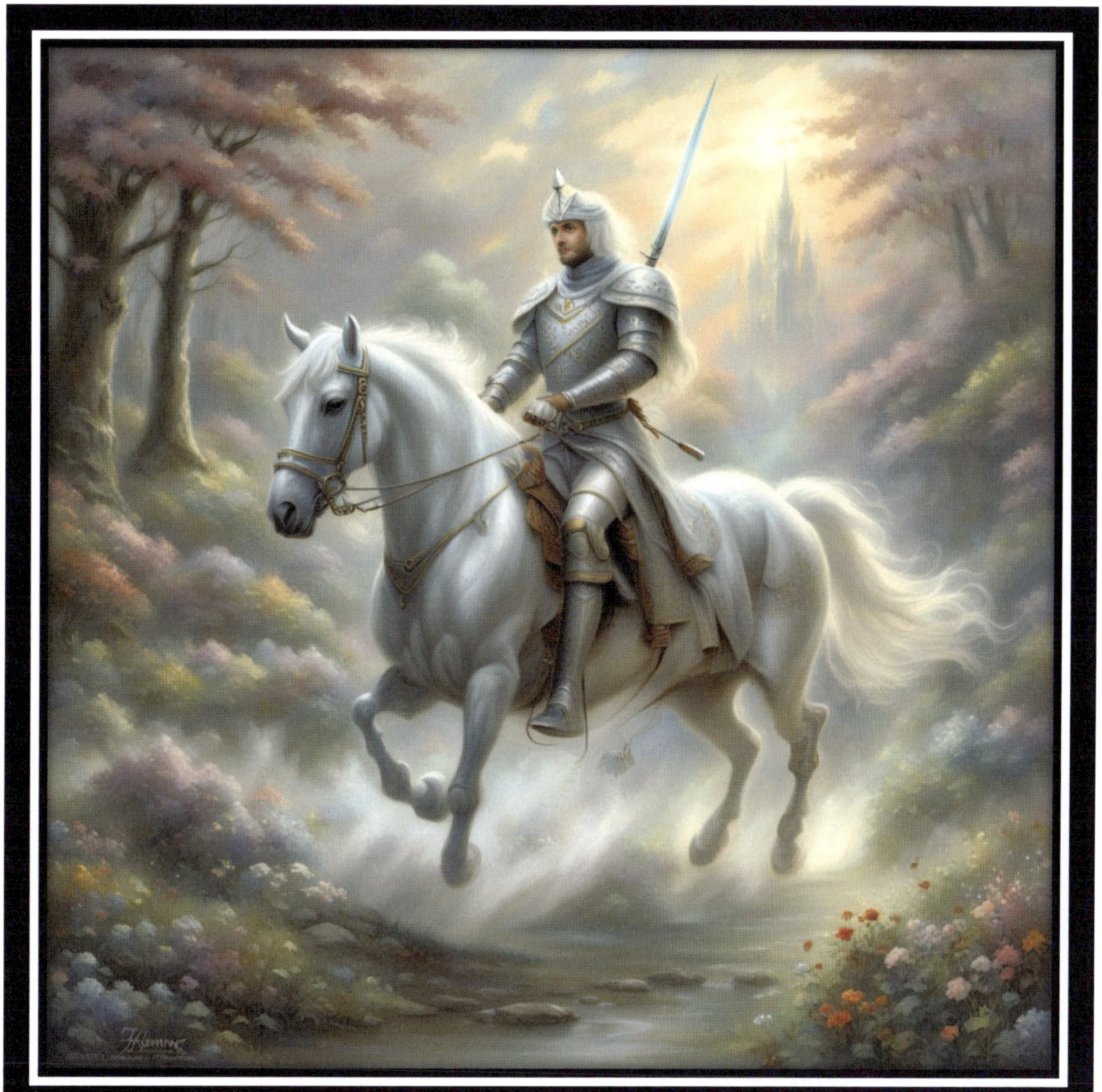

Forty-Eight

By Fiona Riley

Forty-eight, in a state
feeling frumpy, body's lumpy
mental beating – must stop eating
for crying out loud, I'm shaped like a cloud

A party, he said, I filled with dread
nothing to wear, no style to my hair
two stone to lose – that's really bad news
need decent attire to hide my spare tyre

Sneak into boutique, leave feeling a freak
nothing to fit, not even a bit
feel even bigger – as shop girls snigger
we don't have *that* size. Hot tears fill my eyes.

Under duress, the Do's fancy dress
suddenly inspired, no diet required
worrying ended - dignity mended
no matter I'm lardy, he's Laurel, I'm Hardy!

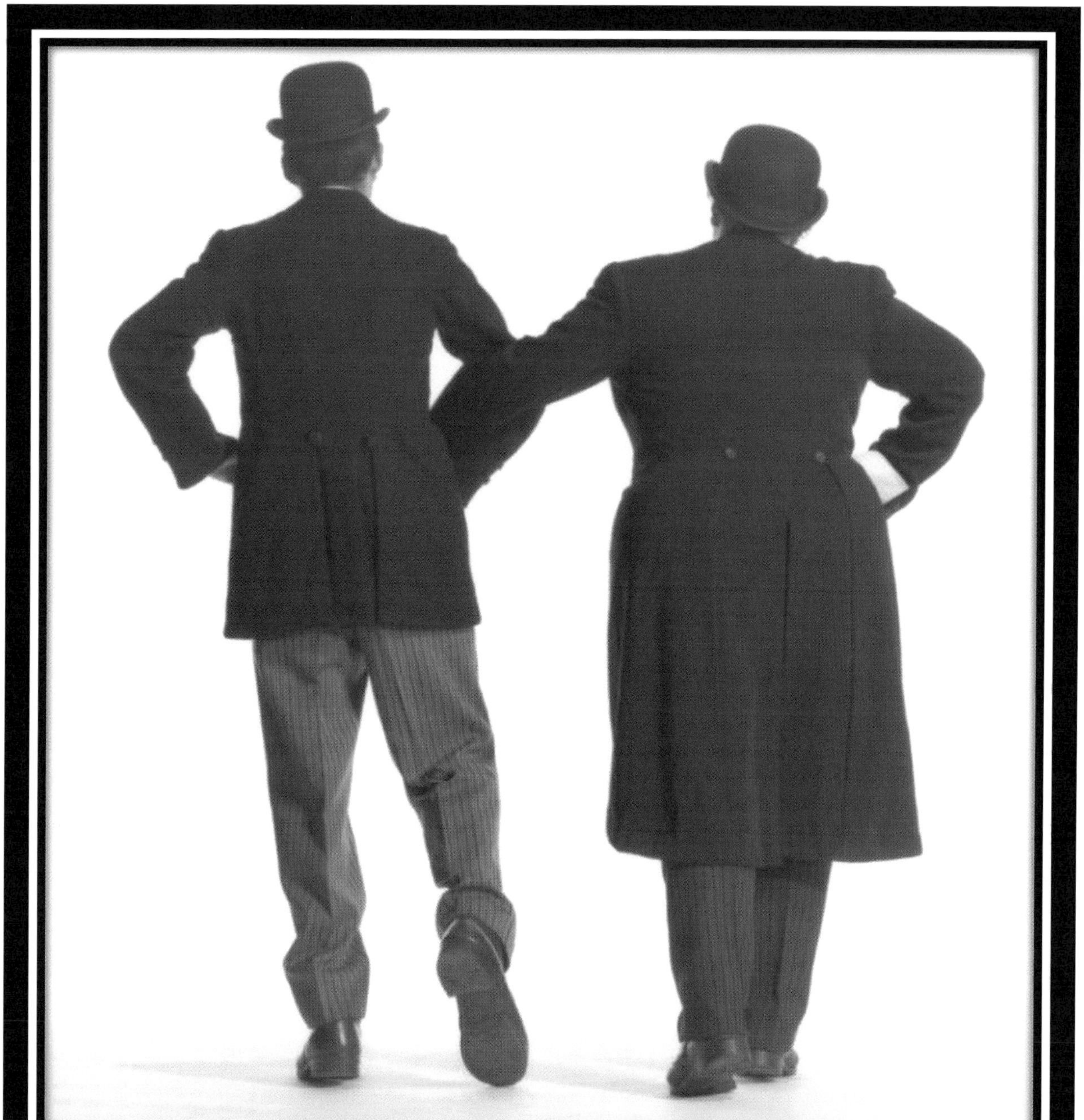

Miss Jennifer Pickles

By Mike Everley

(For the feral cat that shared my writing shed for many years.)

Jennifer Pickles sits on her tail
contemplating the world
and foreign affairs.
Warm in her blanket.
Snug in her box.
Safe in her shed of timber and nails.

Jennifer Pickles sits on her tail.
One ear cocked. One ear flat.
She ruffles her coat.
Black as a coal smudge.
Wise as a judge.
Safe in her shed of timber and nails.

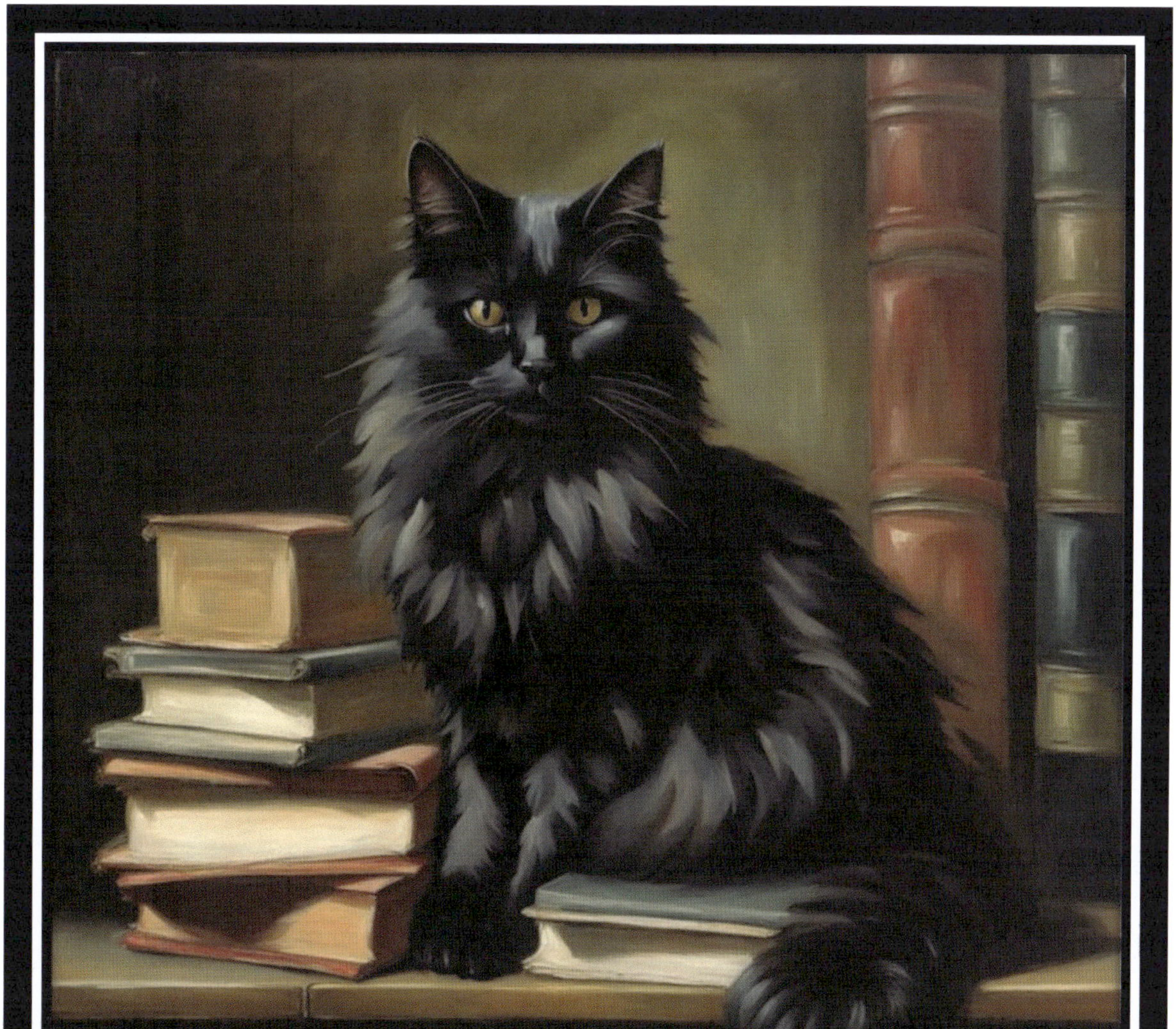

Jennifer Pickles sits on her tail.

Sometimes she feels lonely

and leaps at your lap.

Scattering papers

with kneading claws.

Safe in her shed of timber and nails.

Jennifer Pickles sits on her tail.

Sometimes she's disgruntled

and sits with her back

arched in a comma.

Fluffed up with fur.

Safe in her shed of timber and nails.

Jennifer Pickles sits on her tail

contemplating her mood

for the coming hour.

A hissy, spitty,

yet purry cat.

Safe in her shed of timber and nails.

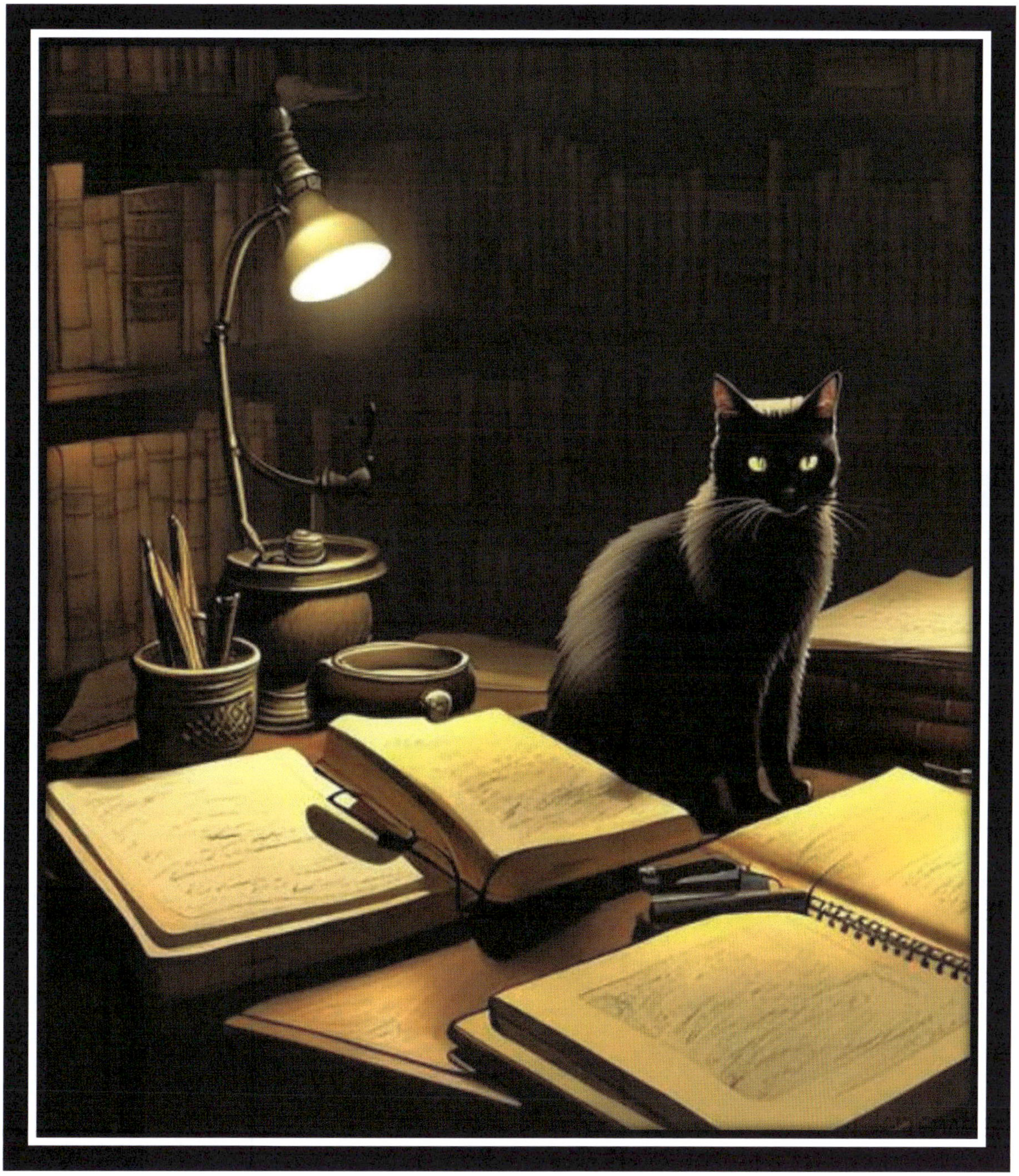

Changing Seasons

By Paula Montez

Do you remember when

The robin and the wren

Sang loudly in the morn

To hail the solstice dawn?

One greeting, one goodbye

Beneath the changing sky,

Each paying their respects,

One season to the next.

In Celtic mythology

The robin represents winter

The wren represents summer

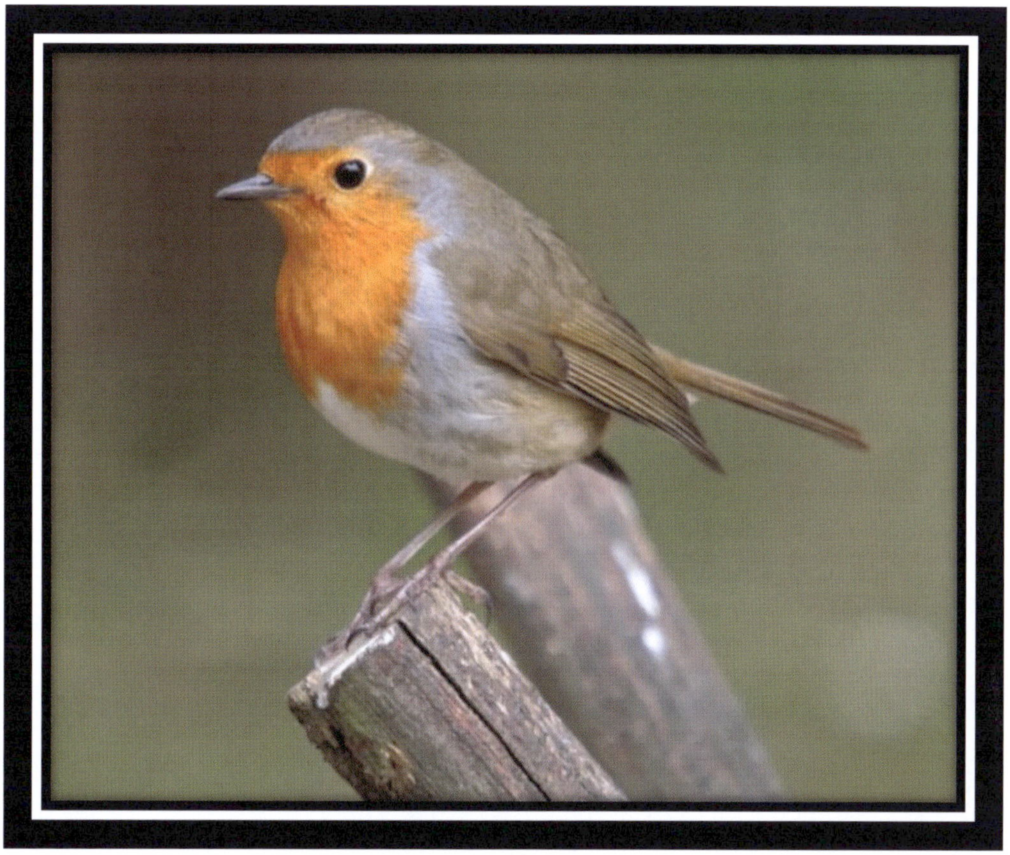

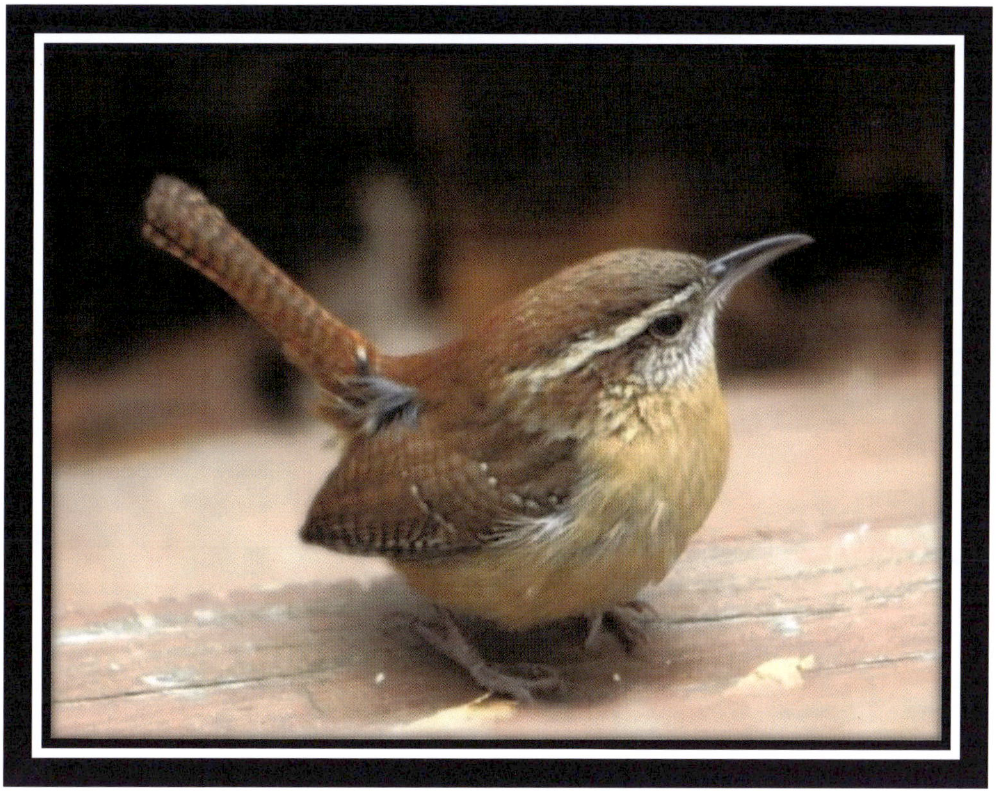

Manic Panic

By Fiona Riley

Feeling manic, in a panic

a poem to write by Monday night.

First person in style, this may take a while,

derangement included (someone's deluded)!

To make matters worse, this attempt at a verse

cannot be rhyme - what a mountain to climb.

Oh golly, begorrah, oh heck, shock and horror

If today is Sunday, then tomorrow is MONDAY

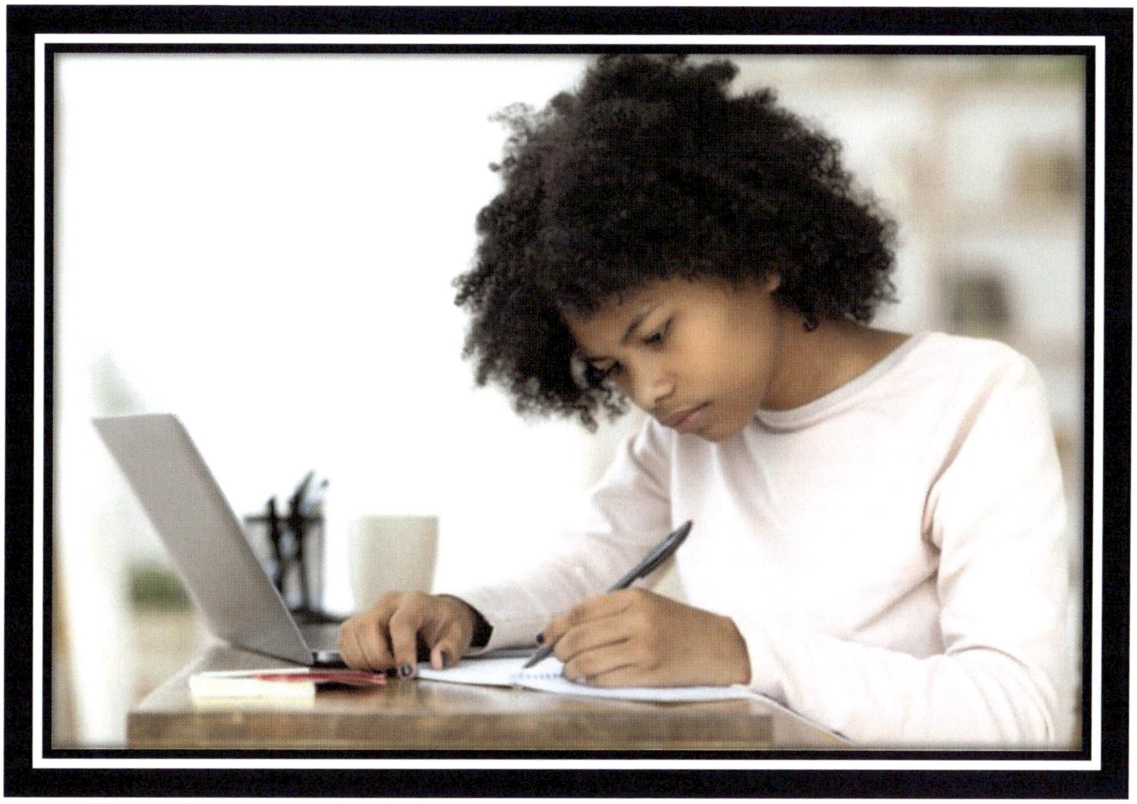

Sometimes I'm wise

By Fiona Riley

Sometimes I'm wise and sometimes I'm not
Sometimes I feel like I've just lost the plot
On occasion I'm clever, but that's almost never
As mostly I know that I know not a lot

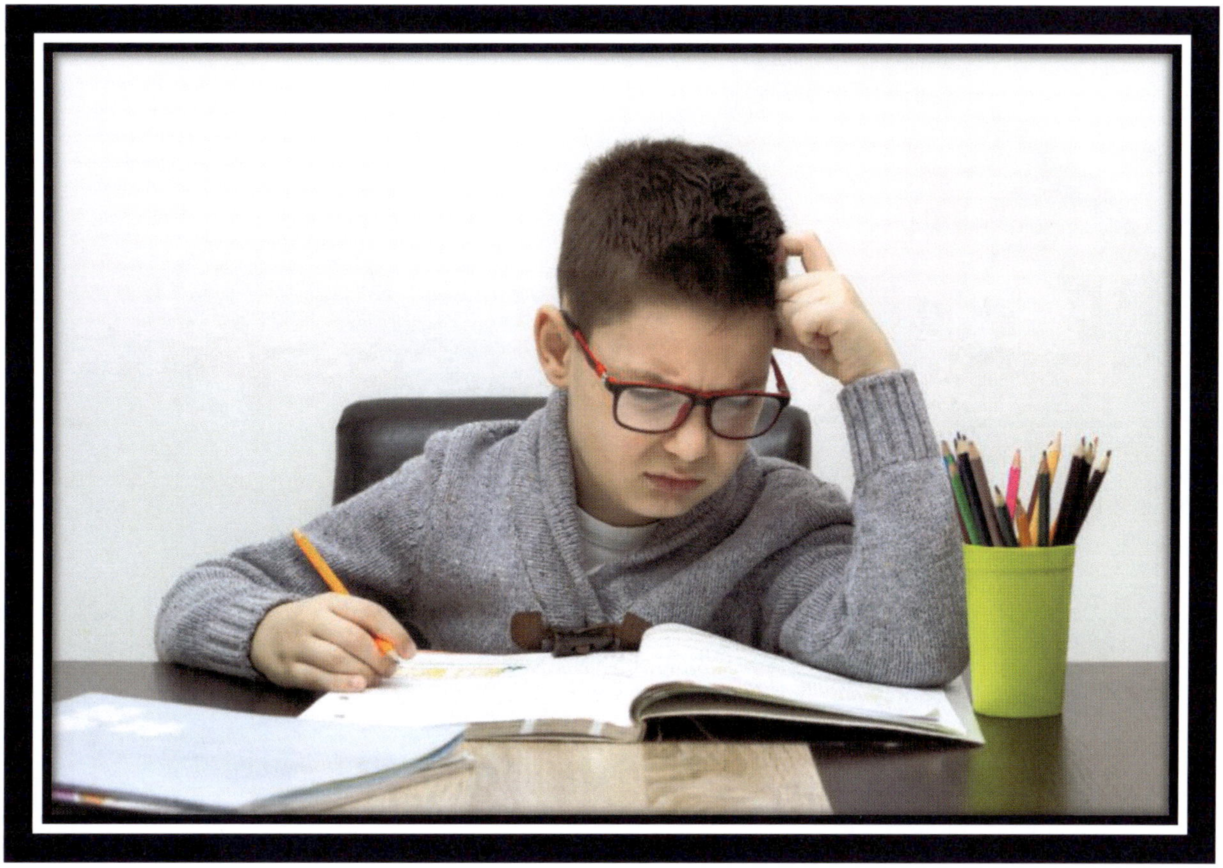

Monkey Business

By Paula Montez

My head is full of monkeys,
There is mischief in the air.
I'm chewing on my pencil,
I am swinging on my chair.

I'll decorate my glasses
To resemble Elton John.
I've got a whoopee cushion
For my boss to sit upon.

I'll wear my Christmas jumper
Even though it's mid-July,
Then eat a juicy currant
And pretend that it's a fly.

I'll gather yellow post-its
To cover all the seating
Then I'm bursting into song
At every business meeting.

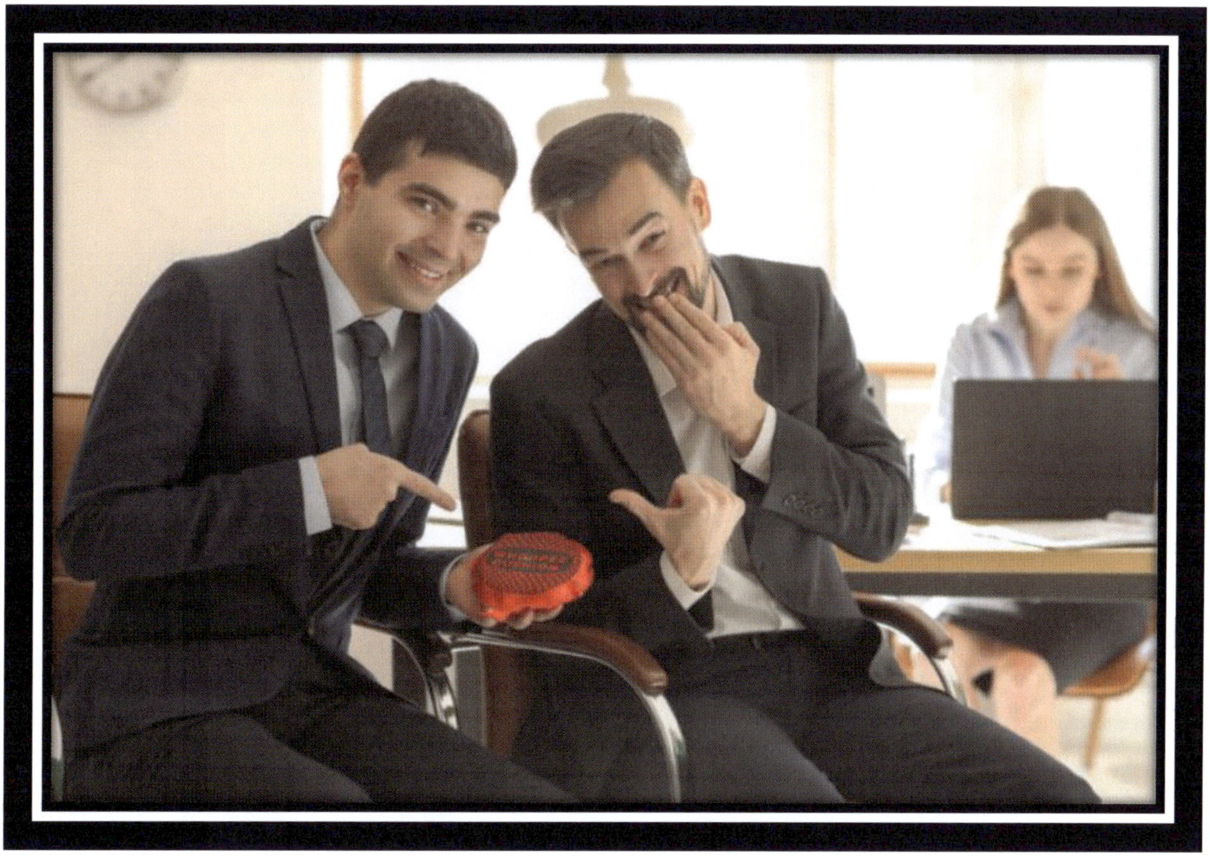

I will phone you up and bark

Just to catch you unawares,

Then skip right through the office

While I swivel all your chairs.

My head is full of monkeys

And I think I know what's wrong.

I'm suffering from Zoomies -

I've worked from home too long!

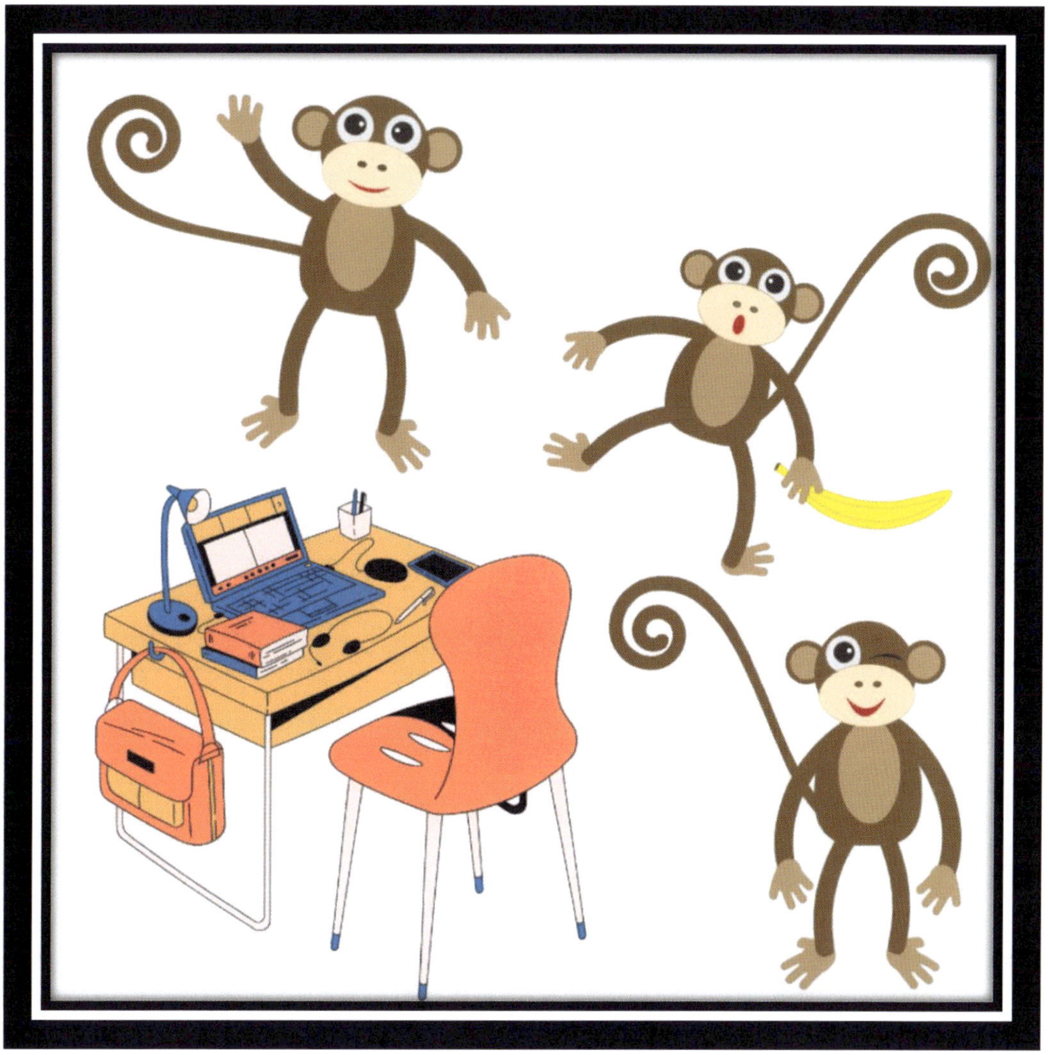

Choices

By Paula Montez

We all walk different paths,

Please don't judge the one I choose

Even if I tread unwisely,

Even if I trip and bruise.

For I won't have lost the lesson,

And I'll realign my boots,

I won't be heading backwards,

I'll recalculate my route.

If we all chose but one path

That flows without a hitch,

We would wear it down with trudging –

It would end up as a ditch.

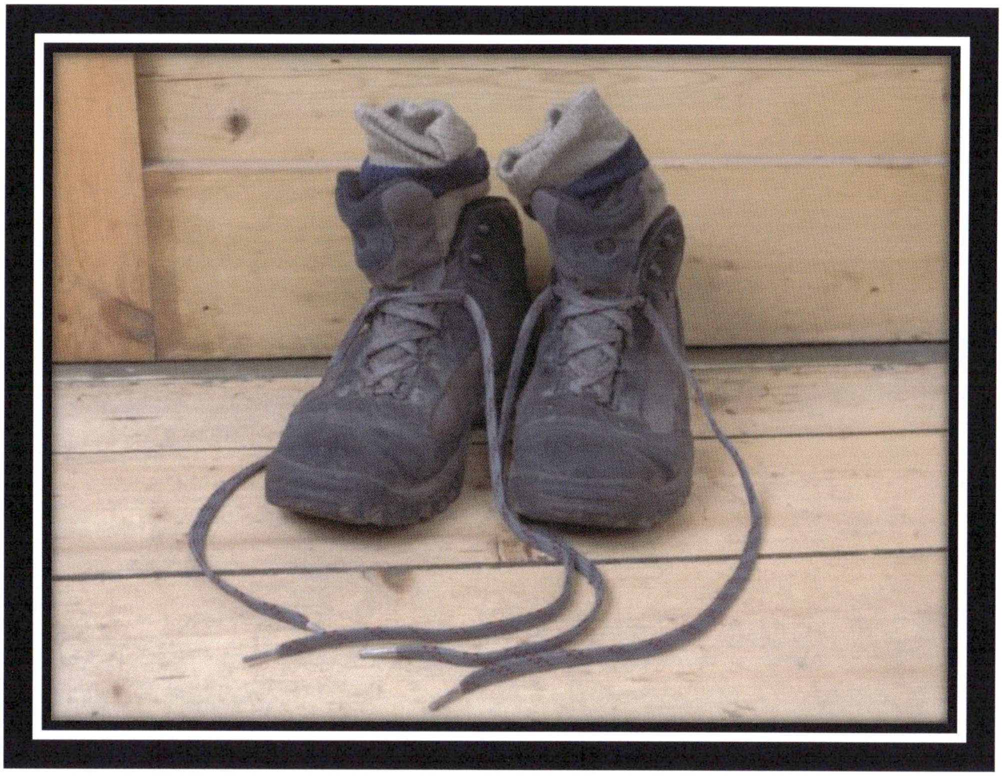

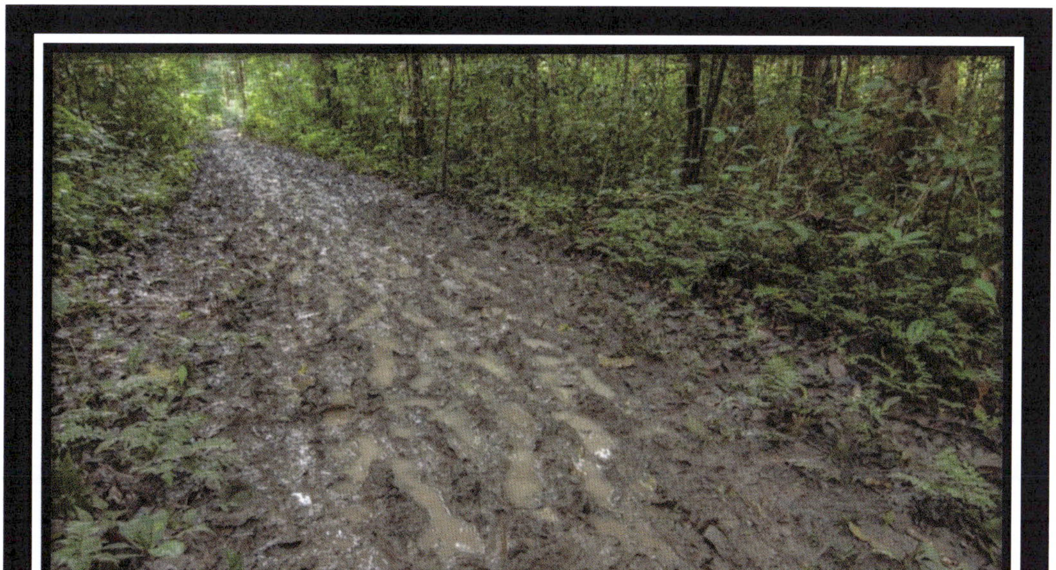

Sunset with Cows

By Mike Everley

There's something quite romantic
about sunsets and cows
don't you think?

Is it just me that loves their quiet moods
while strolling home from the pub
after a drink?

They stand there nonchalant and shake their heads
as I stumble on my way....
Sometimes they wink.

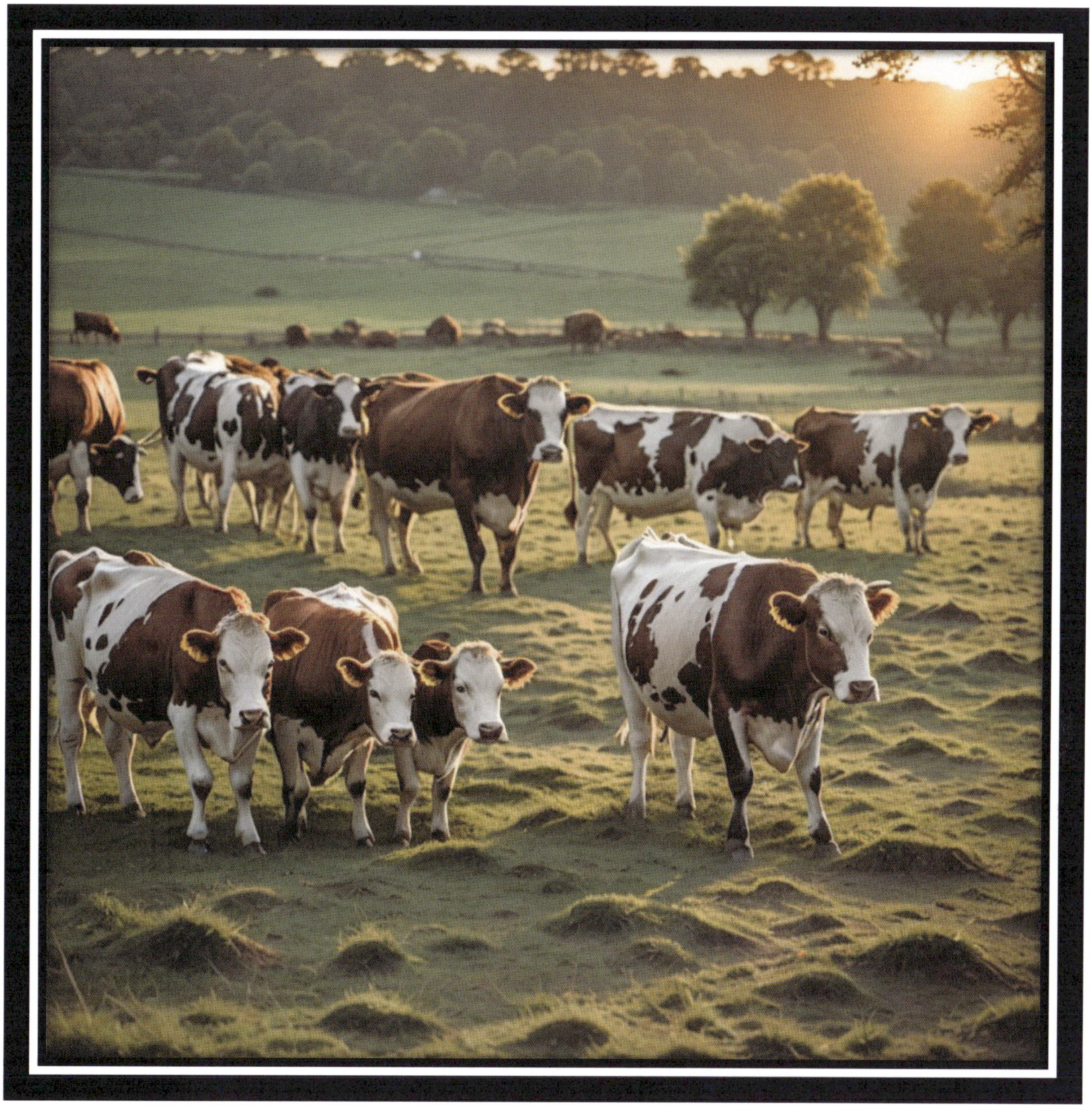

Water Mill at Dunster Castle, Somerset

By Mike Everley

Harnessed together,

water on wood,

elemental power.

Mill wheel turning,

driving, revolving,

slowly grinding

stone ground flour

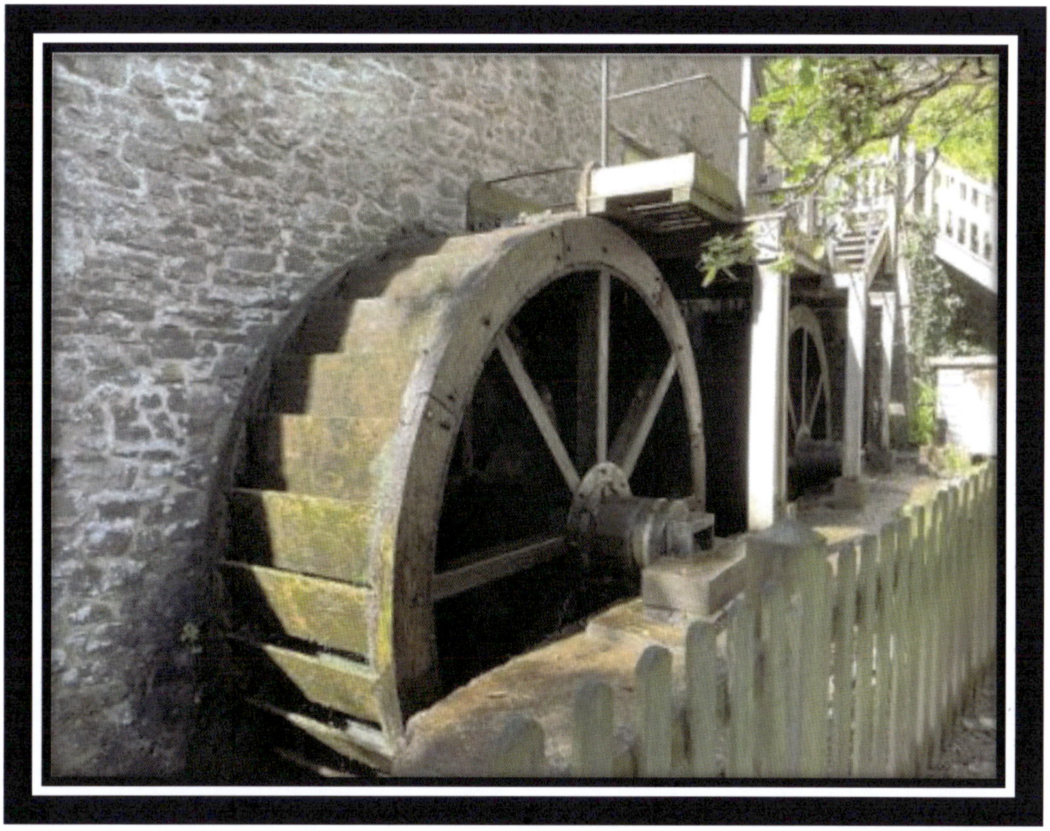

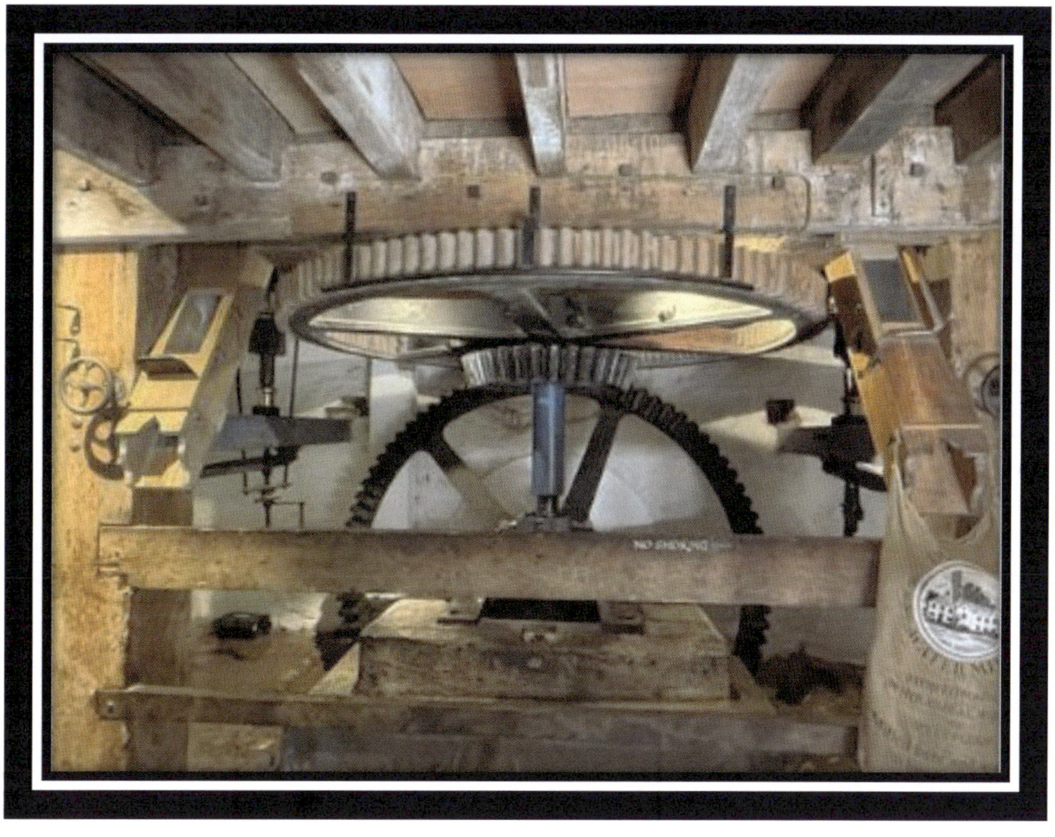

The Chosen One

By Paula Montez

Twenty people in the room
All gathered round for tea,
The cat walked in, perused the crowd,
And from them all chose me!

You can guess that I felt special,
Each person was assessed,
Her piercing eyes made judgement
And 'twas I who passed the test.

She turned her back on outstretched hands,
Her haughty head held high,
Sauntered over, flicked her tail
Then nestled on my thigh.

And there she purred, contented,
What more could someone wish,
But I doubt that I am special -
I just smell a bit like fish!

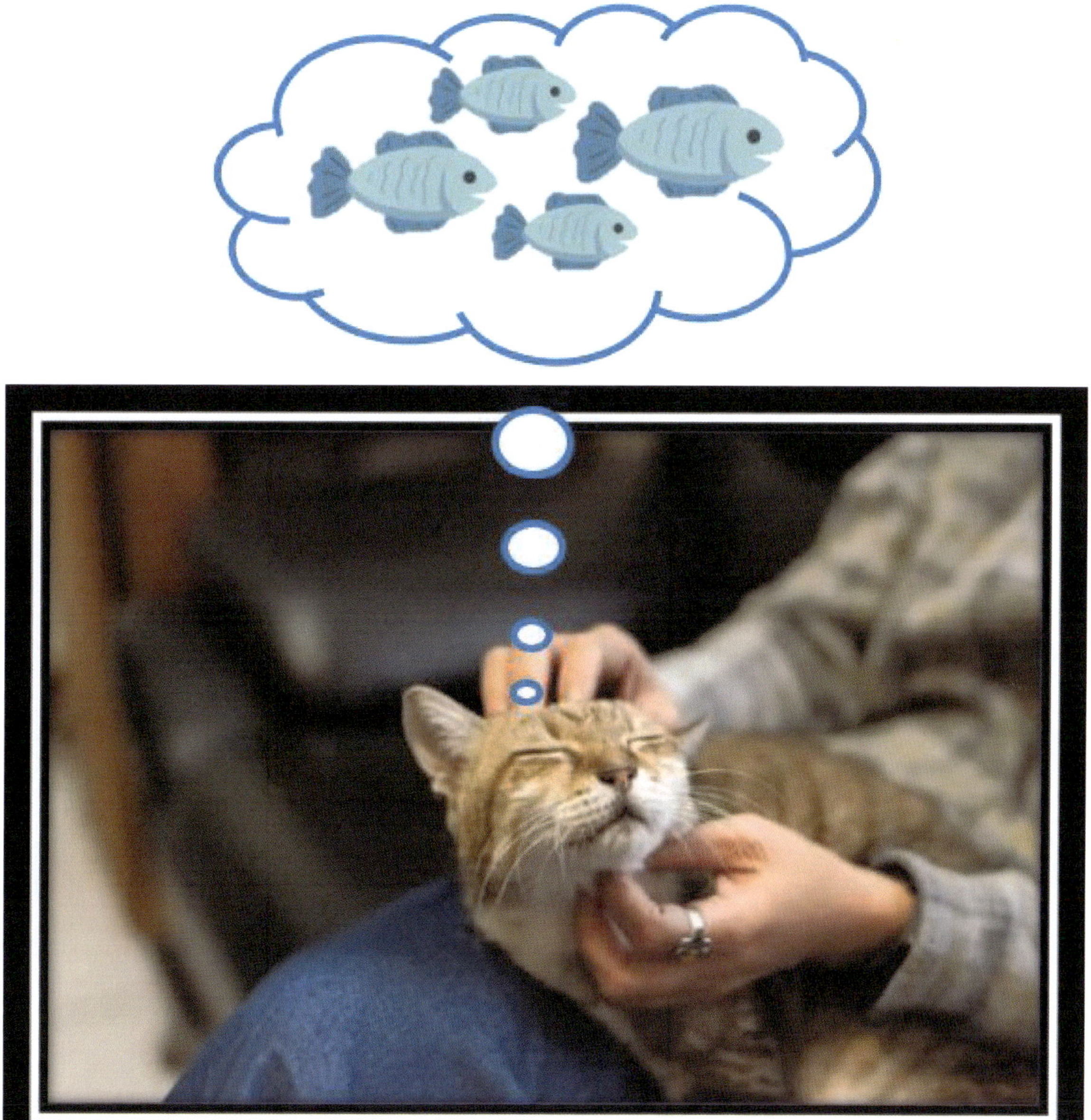

Apple Blossom

By Mike Everley

Frail transient beauty

subject to the vagaries

of wind and weather.

Petals fall randomly

after sudden storms,

littering confetti

on grass and paths.

Short lived they die

in soft curls,

only, like hope, to return

the following year.

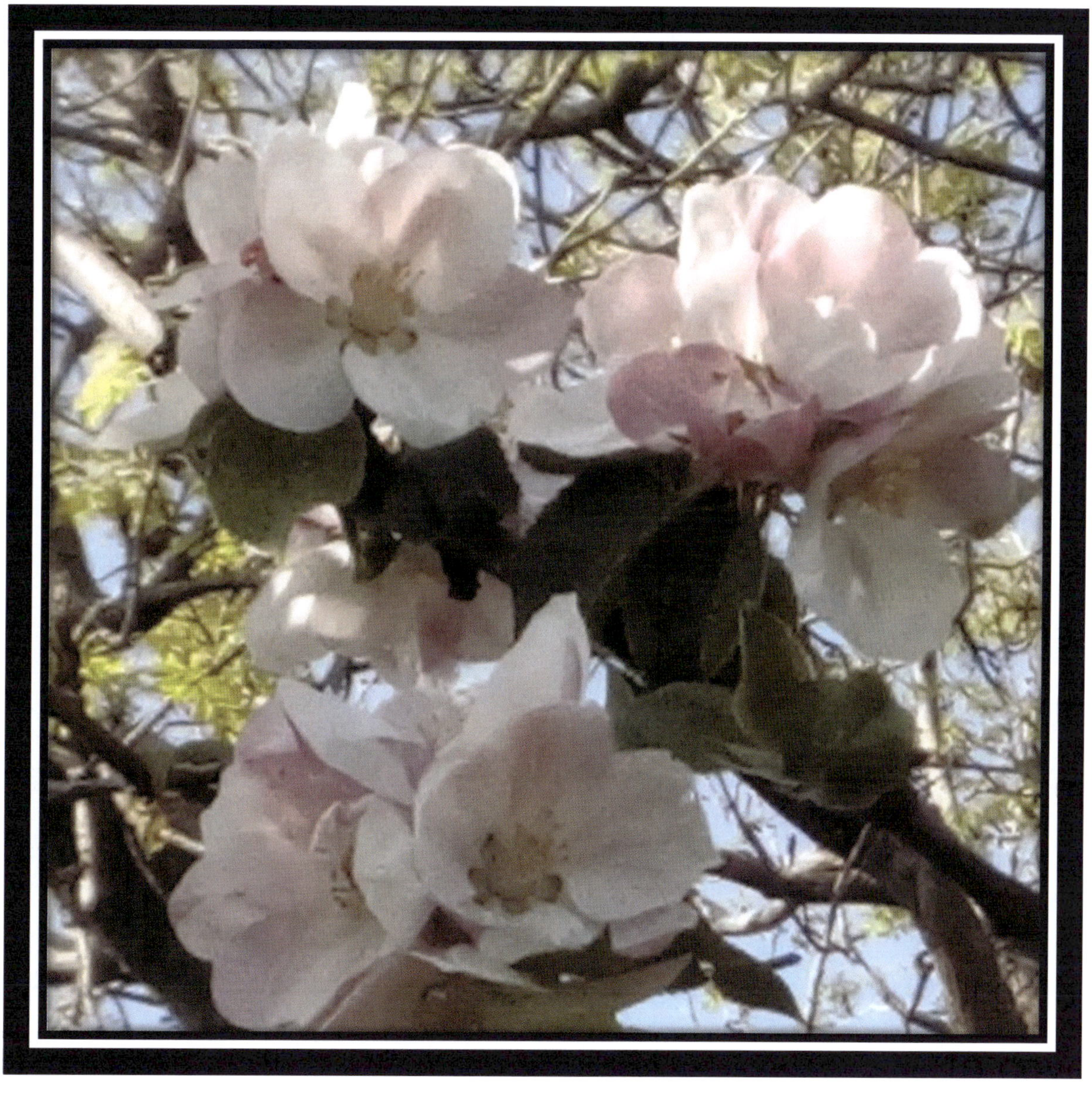

Snowdrop

By Paula Montez

The Snowdrop glistens on the slope
Through icy soil her buds unfold,
Yet uncomplaining of the cold,
Her petals hold the springtime hope.

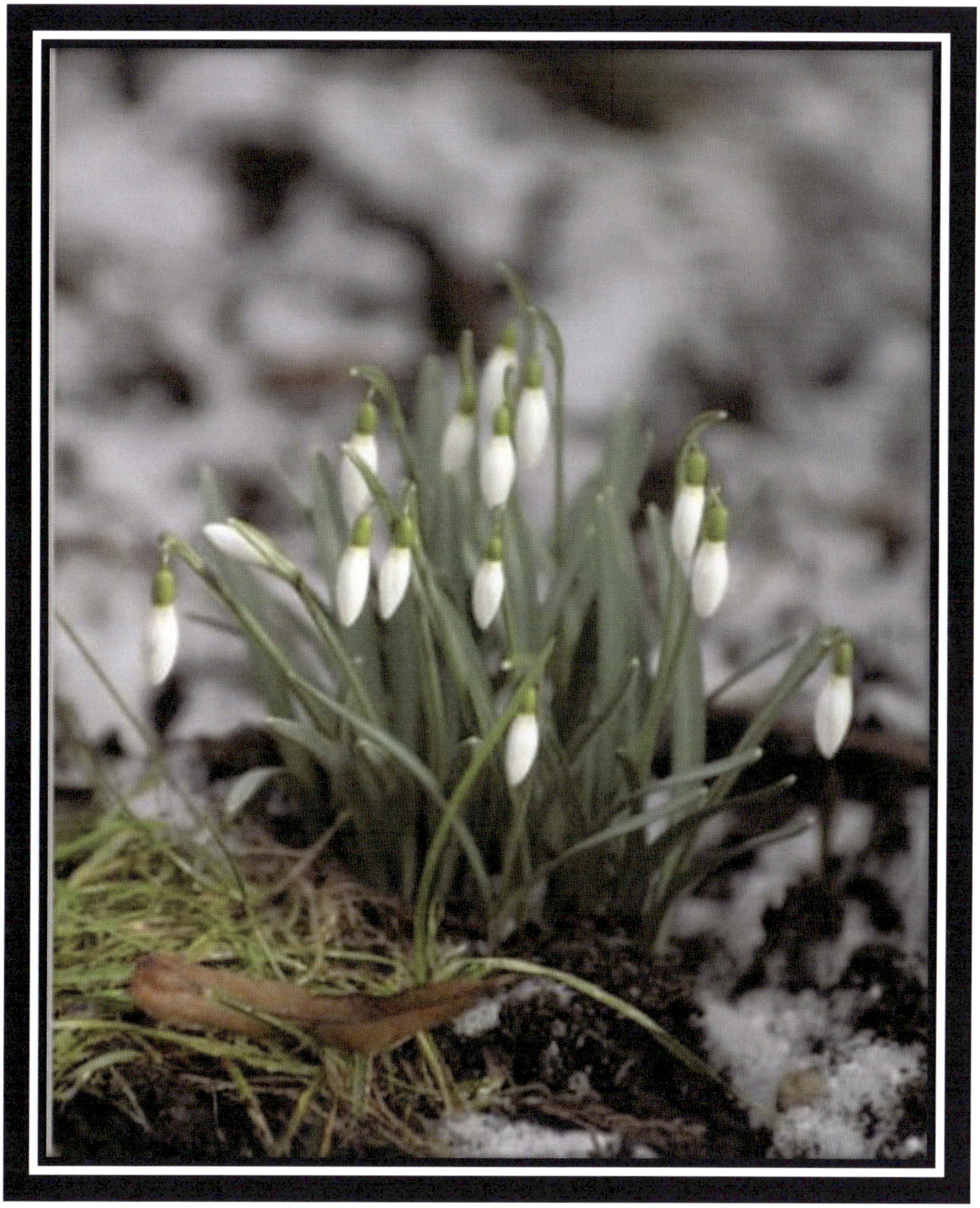

Sea Feverish

By Ann Marie Thomas

I must go down to the seas again,
To the lonely sea and the sky,
And all I need is a tall ship
And a star to steer her by.

With air conditioning, all mod cons,
And the sea like a millpond still.
'Cause if it were to pitch about
I surely would get ill.

I must go down to the seas again,
But only if the weather's nice.
I'm not one for wind-blown hair
Or hands as cold as ice.

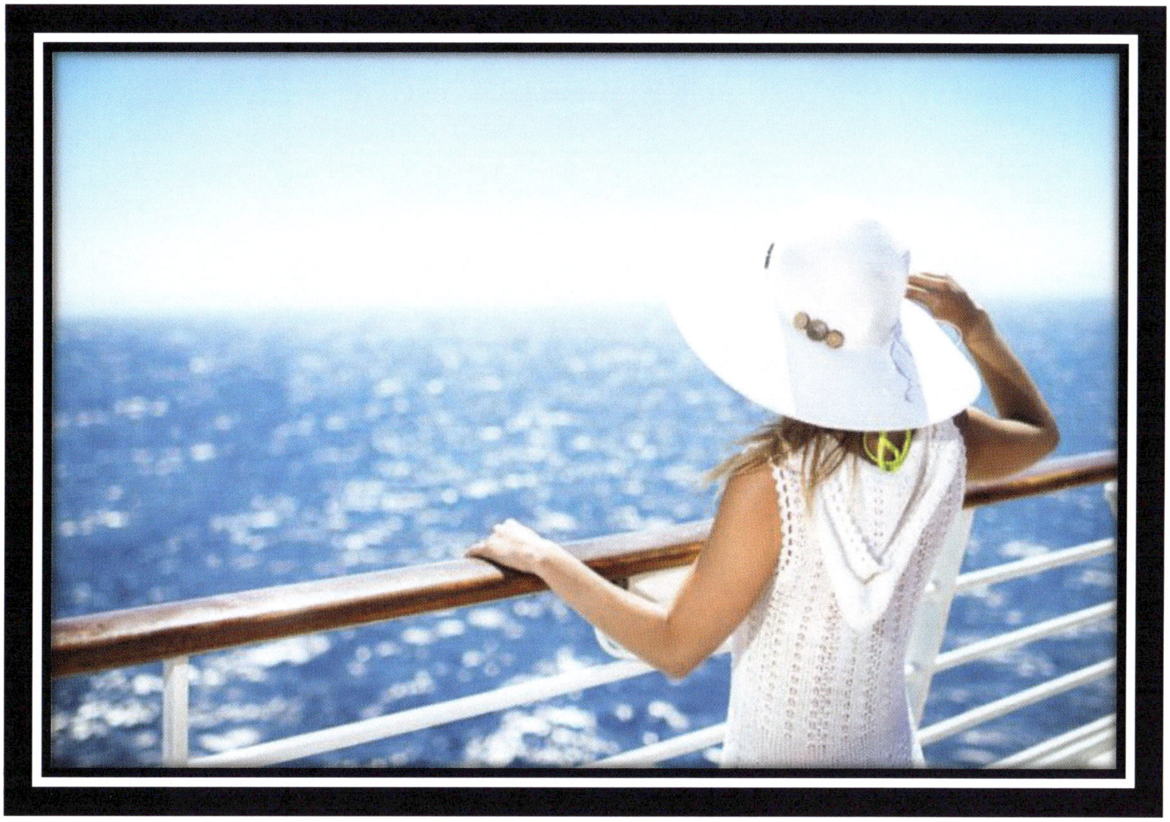

And all I need is a tall ship

With thirteen decks at least,

With non-stop entertainment,

And every night a feast.

I think John Masefield had it right,

I haven't had a break in ages.

I'll just get out my smartphone

And Google Yellow Pages.

(Inspired by John Masefield's poem 'Sea-Fever')

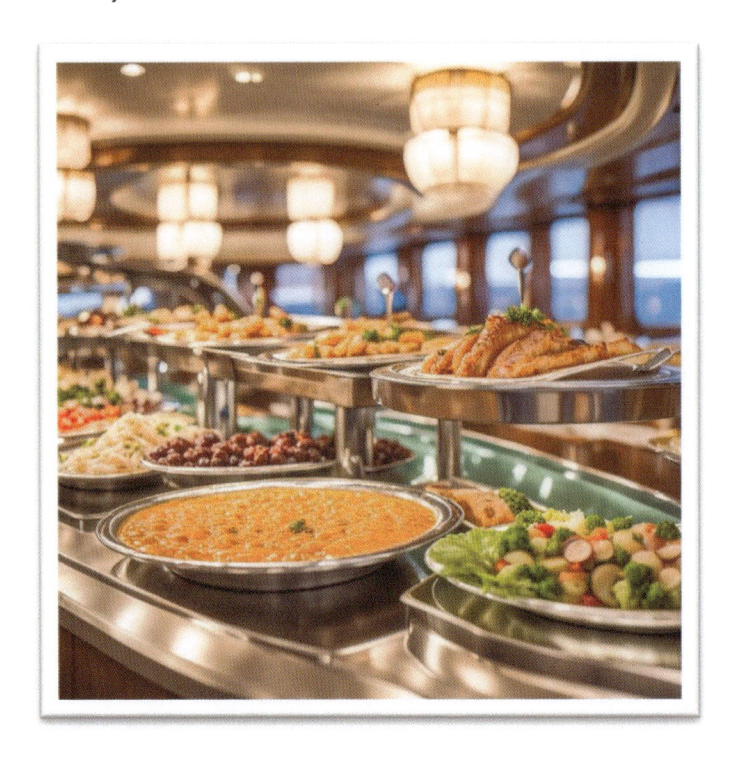

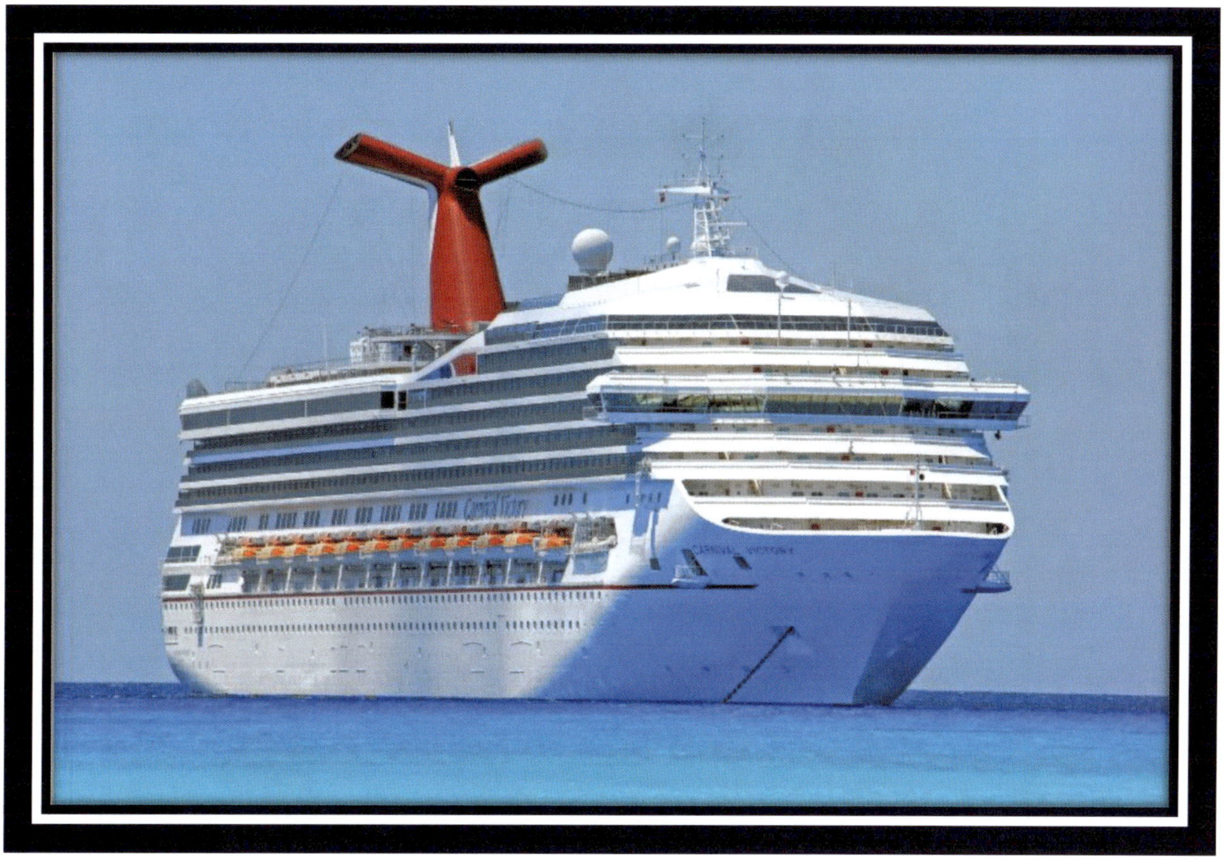

Goodbye, Arkwright

By Rhydderch Wilson

Goodbye, Arkwright
Goodbye, old friend
Farewell to you and your old corner shop
Where you stood on duty from dawn until dark
With your tin cans piled high in dusty old corners
Where fog-horn voiced fishwives would stop for a chat
To buy string and boot polish and food for the cat

Goodbye, neighbours
I hope you're all well
Remember the days when we lived in the streets
The pavements awash with gossip and bikes
Everyone feeding everyone's kids
The grannies and grandpas looked out for by all
I knew all your names and you knew mine

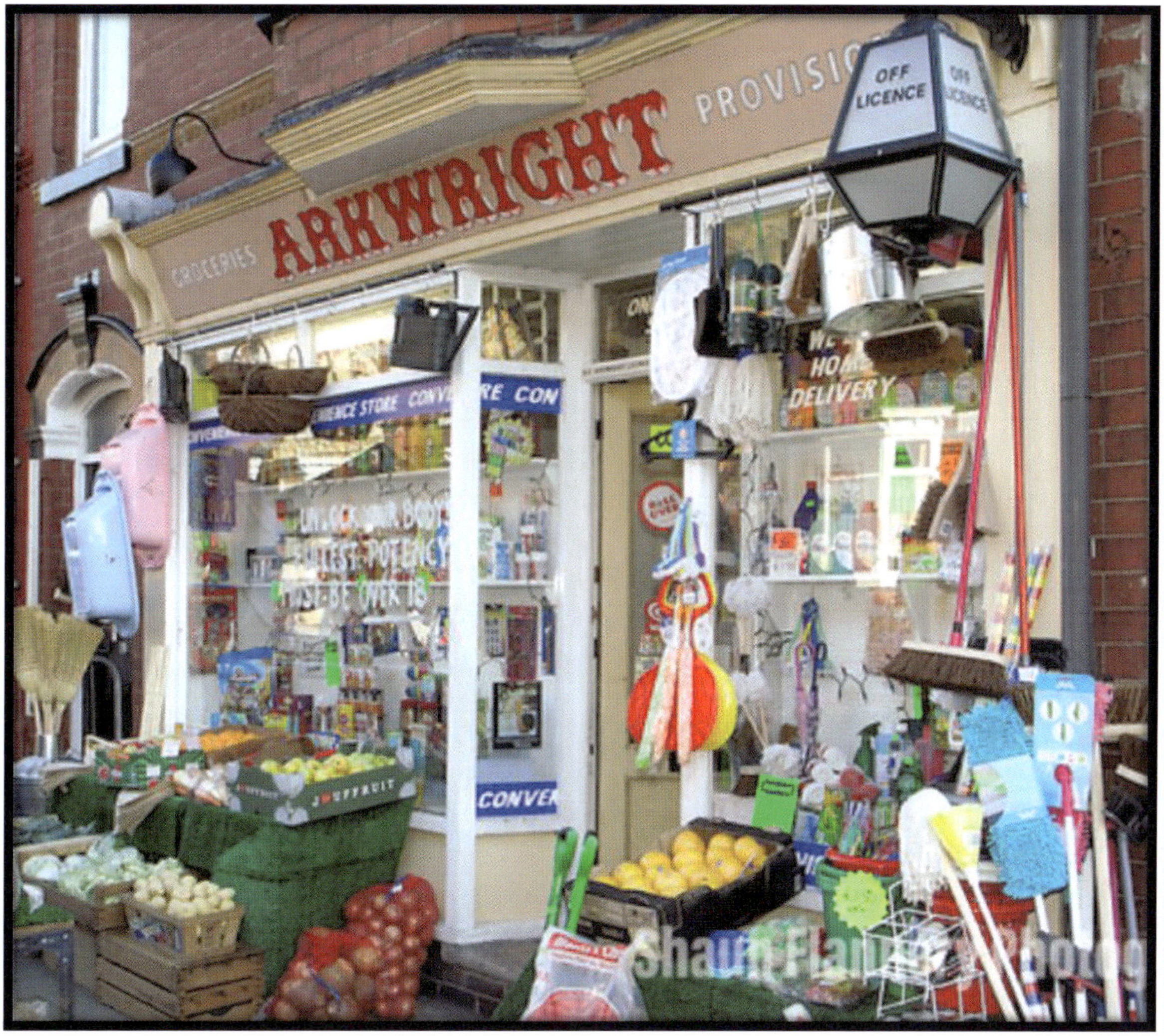
GROCERIES
ARKWRIGHT
OFF LICENCE
OFF LICENCE

Goodbye, children

It's time to move on

Those were the days we were always outdoors

With mothers on doorsteps keeping an eye

Footballs and bikes and dens in the gardens

Friendly old neighbours and welcoming houses

How quickly we'd scarper when a window was smashed

Goodbye to my local

Where have you gone?

I'd like to visit just one last time

For a quiet pint with my friends in the snug

Dirt covered shift-workers mumbling softly

Politics, strikes, football and kids

And the rain lashing against your frosted windows

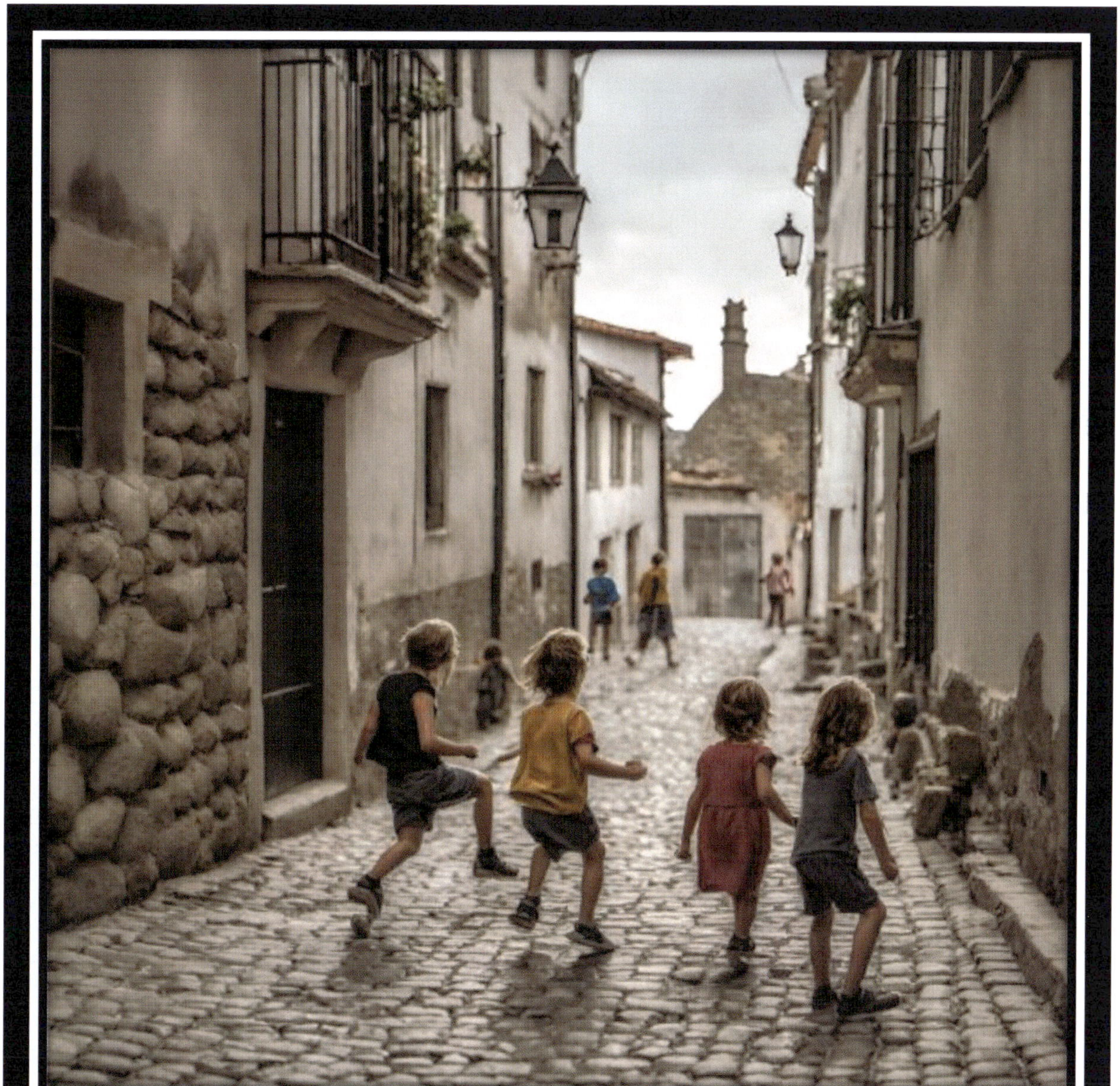

Goodbye, mister coal man

I remember you well

You'd come every Thursday to fill up our shed

With the old rag n bone man not far behind

With his hoary old horse and familiar cry

We visited once, your cobbled old trove

So much treasure for a little boy's eyes

Goodbye to you, street parties

My favourite times

Grainy old films of fancy dressed kids

Cowboys and soldiers and nurses and devils

With bunting and fairy-cakes on wallpaper tables

Games and races and prizes for all

Nobody cared about the occasion

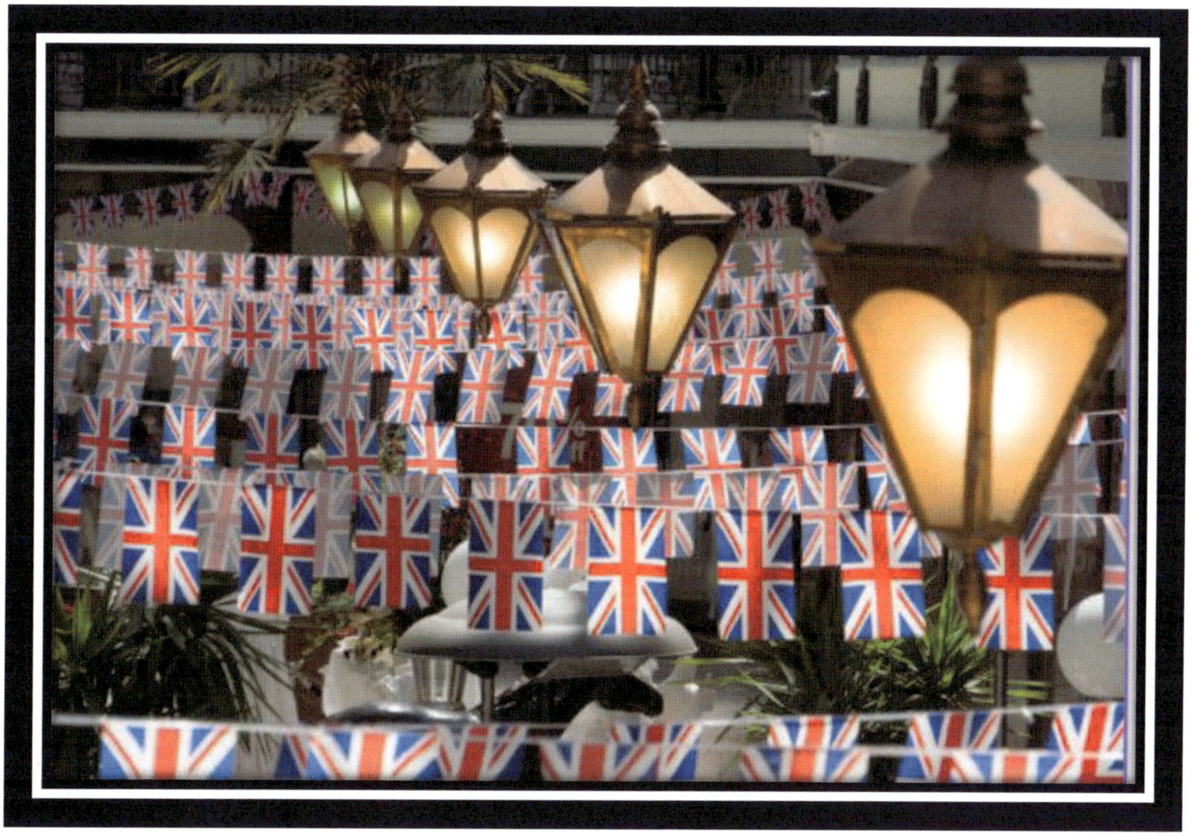

Goodbye, Arkwright

Goodbye, old friend

Someone's decided it's time to go

I wish you could stay, I'm sorry you can't

Someone's decided you're needed no more

Goodbye, Arkwright

Goodbye, old friend

I miss you more than you'll ever know

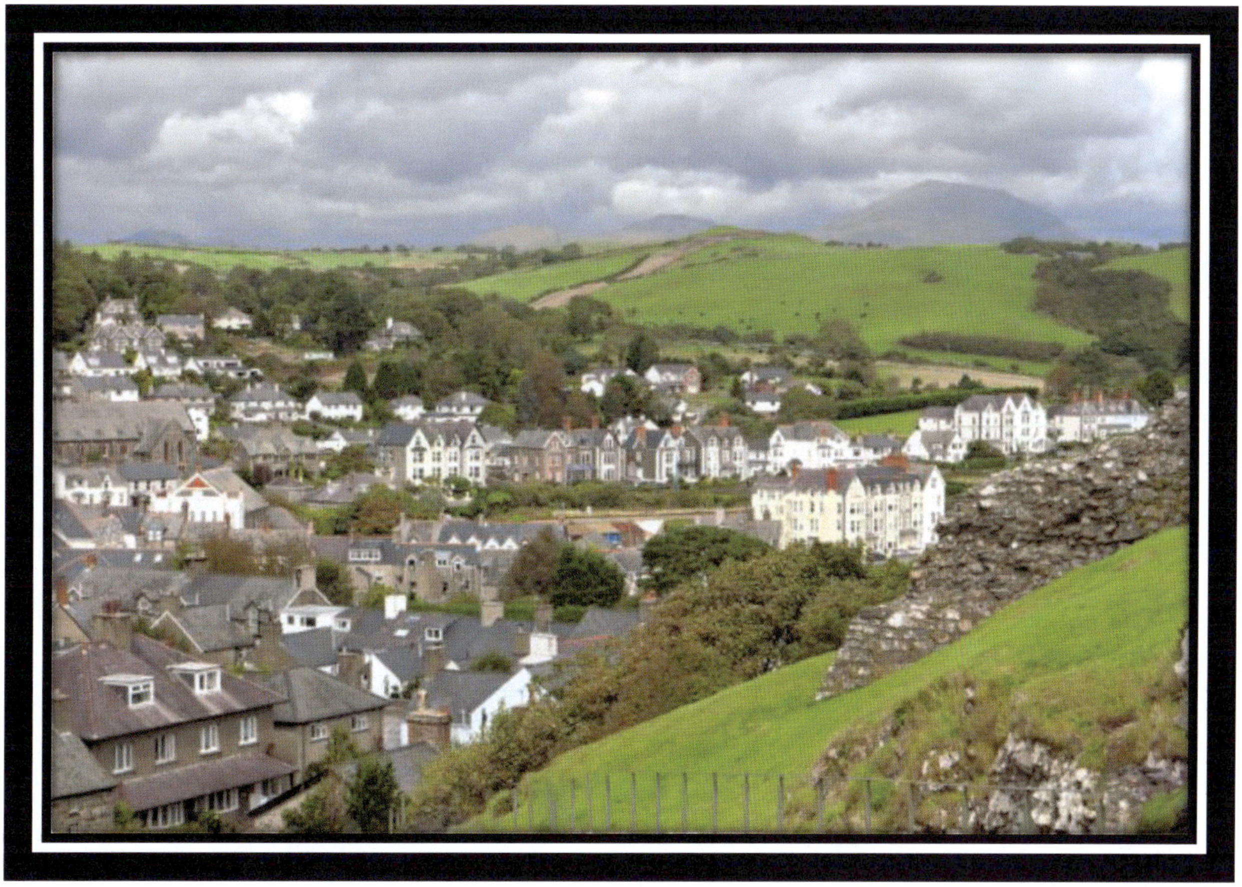

James Bond
By Paula Montez

> The name is Bond, James Bond.
>
> I brought a peace offering for you, Dr. No.
>
> Here's a packet of *Dreamies* for your cat.

Aha, Mr. Bond, I've been expecting you. One pull of this lever, and the trap door to the sharks will open. Are you ready to hand over the *Dreamies*?

Mirror

By Joan Darbyshire

Who's that in there? He stares, I stare.

But I don't care,

'Cos I am bold,

His gaze I'll hold.

His nose is cold

So I can tell

He must be well.

He's got no smell,

I'll move my paw. I'm sure I saw his paw withdraw.

I turn to flee

And so does he.

My God! He's me!

Who's that　　　　　　in there?
He stares.　　I stare.
But I don't care,
'c●s I am b●ld,
His gaze I'll hold.
His **NOSE** is cold
So I **CAN** tell
He must be well.
He's got no smell !

move my paw. I'm sure I saw His paw with-
I'll /　　　　I turn to flee　　　　　　\ draw.
And so does he.
My God! He's me!

Light Breaks

By Mike Everley

Light breaks

in the high kingdom

beneath a brooding sky

Below the bare mountain tops,

and ragged tree lines

lie draped in white wisps

of fine, damp mist.

A pool of silver-grey water

sits heavy as mercury

in an elbow of granite.

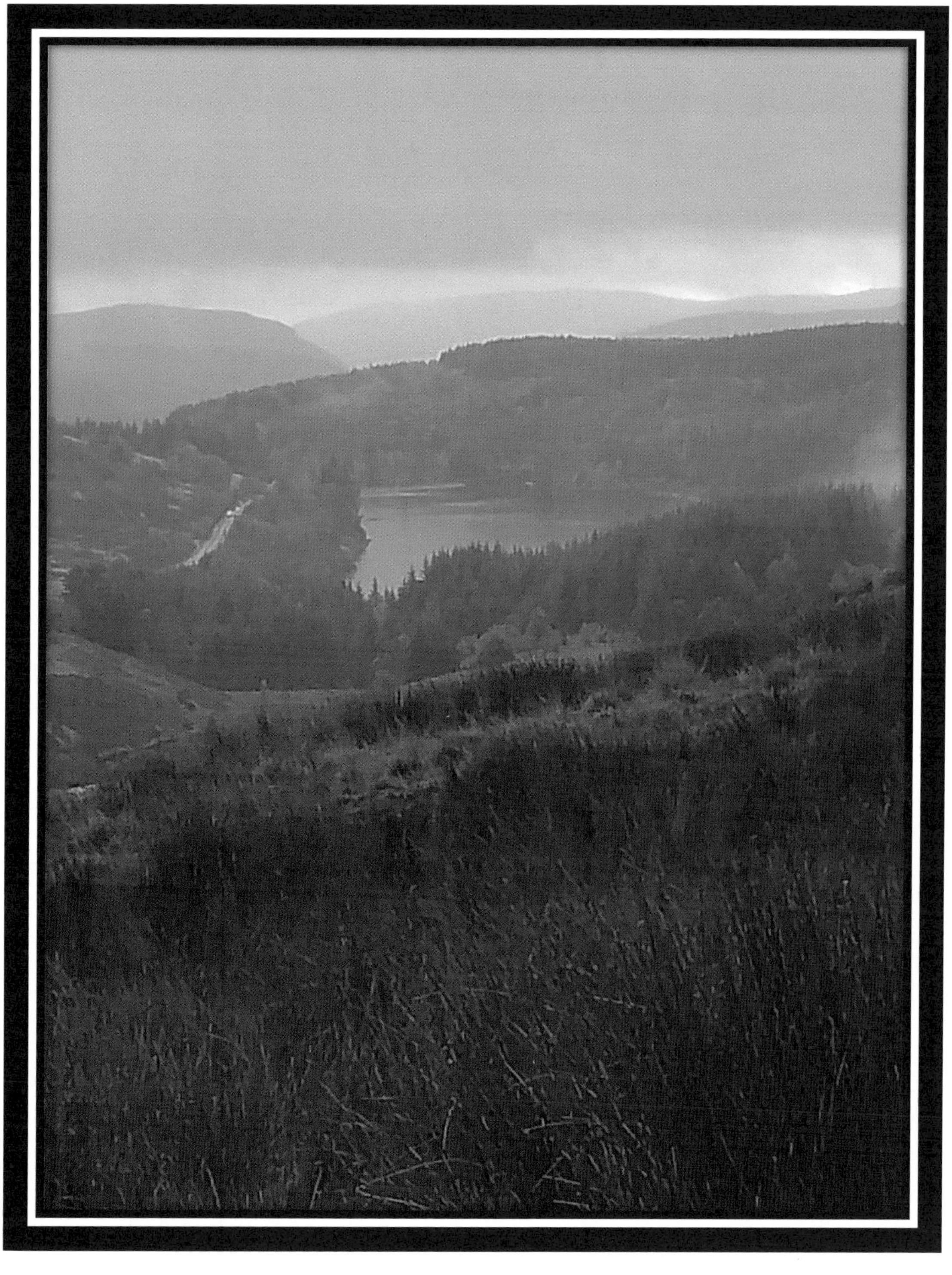

List of Resolutions
By Paula Montez

This year's resolutions - a lifestyle revolution.

Friday night – no Wychwood Ale
Just smoothies made of curly kale.
Give my liver quite a treat,
No more dairy, no more meat,
Cut out everything that's sweet.

Deadlines, finish well before.
Sort those random kitchen drawers.
Darn the holes in all my socks.
30 days of strict detox
(I know that I will miss the chocs).

Get my abs rock-hard and tight,
50 sit-ups every night.
Scour the oven twice a week.
Keep my desk pristine and neat.
Run 'til I'm at peak physique.

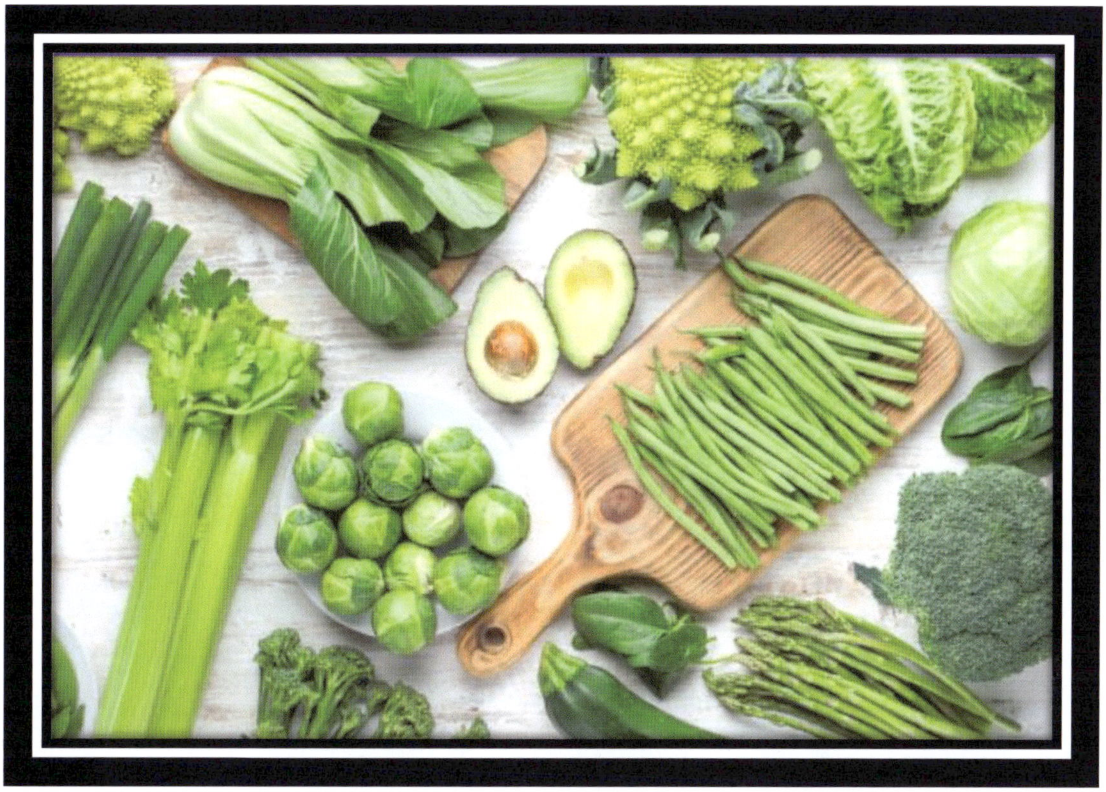

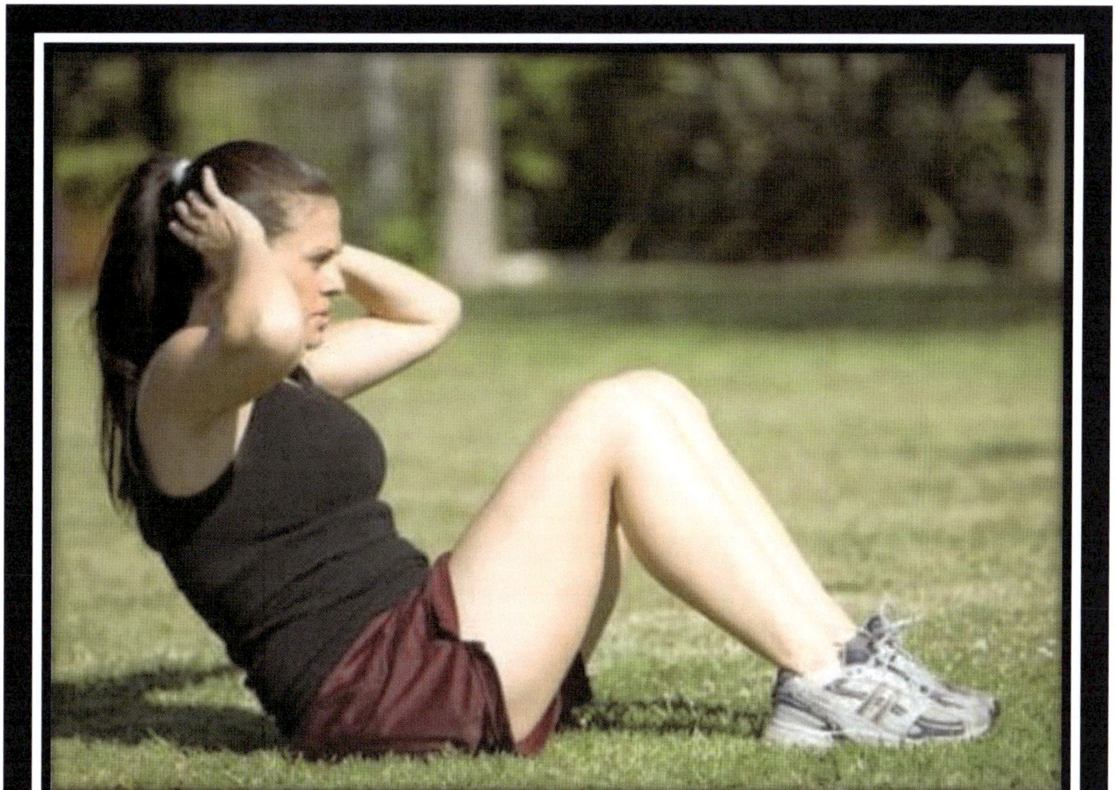

Learn a language, learn to dance.

Don't leave anything to chance.

No more telly – hike instead.

Organise the garden shed.

Cook from scratch, start baking bread.

Oh yes, and one more thing I missed-

Stop writing unachievable lists.

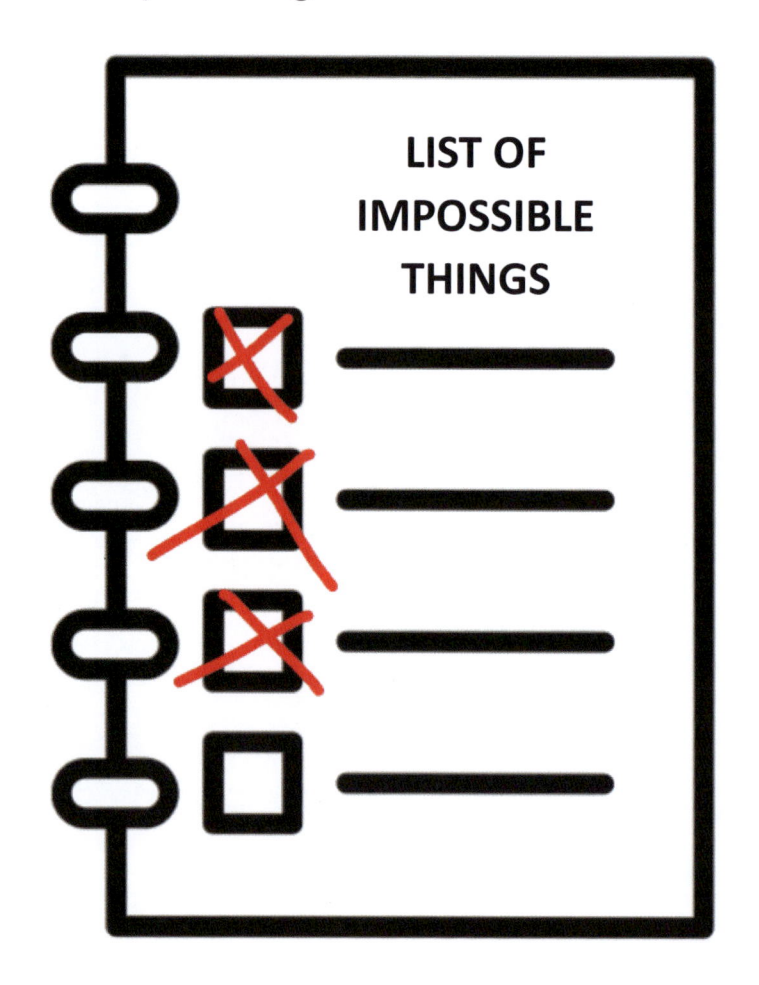

88

Throw It!

By Paula Montez

The wait, the chase - my daily obsession.

This ball, for now, my prized possession.

I leap, I run in joyous rapacity,

Instincts engaged to full capacity.

By teatime forgotten and left behind,

Replacements are always so easy to find.

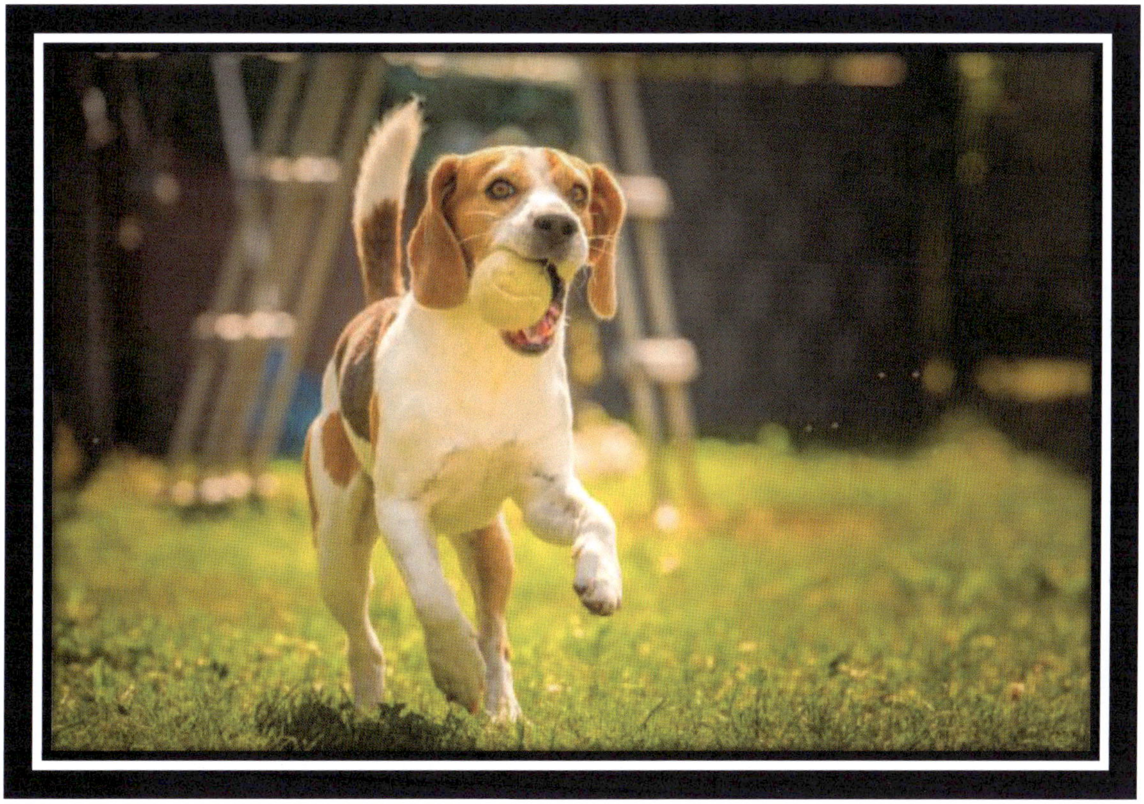

The New Sweep (Changing the idiom)

By Fiona Riley

The new sweep,

brooms clean, sheets pristine,

lays out shiny bright rods.

Spiky round brushes

bristle in anticipation.

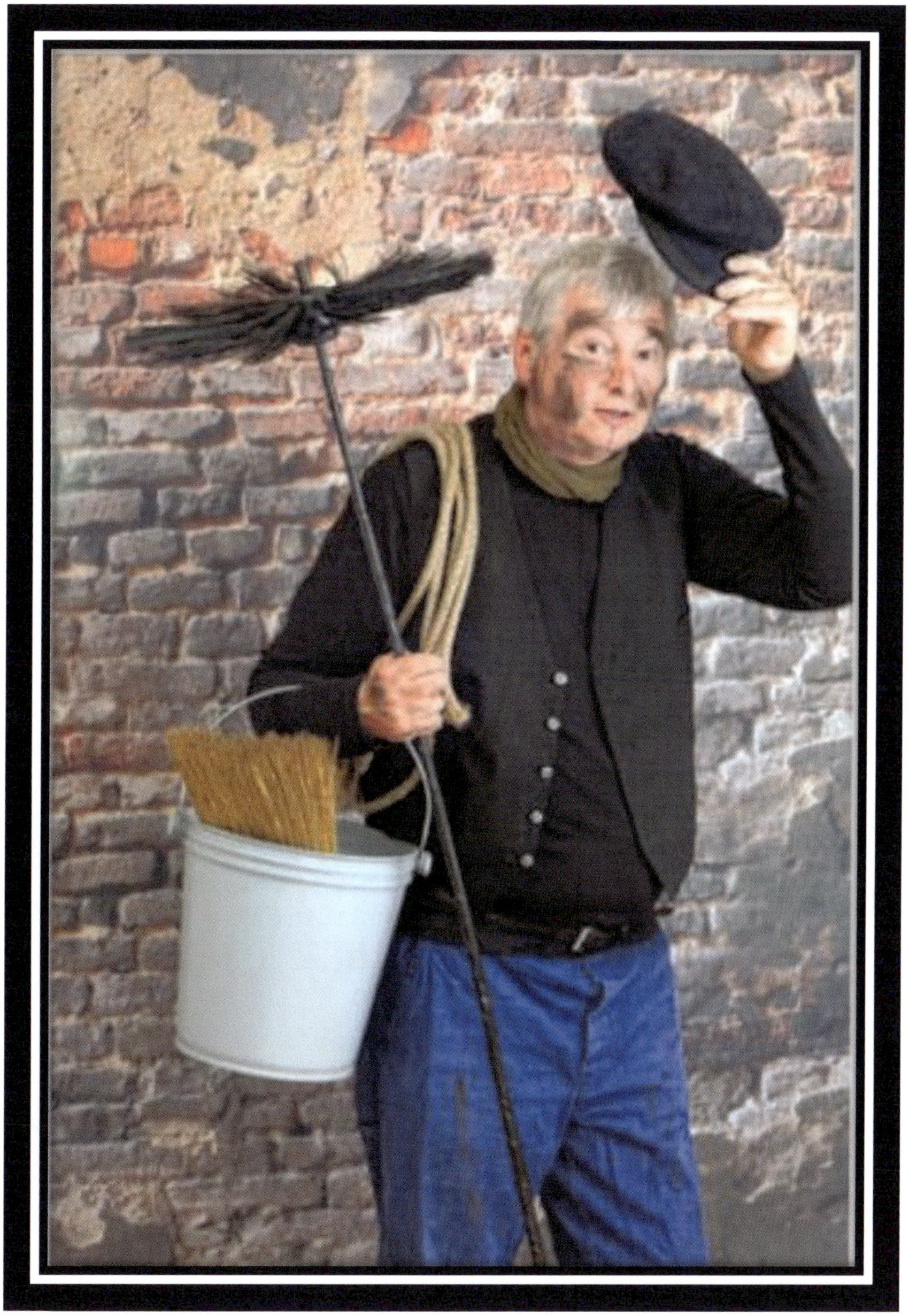

Arthur Bell
By Mike Everley

A very sad story I have to tell
of a young wizard named Arthur Bell.
His spell backfired I'm sad to say.
He turned into a rat that day.

He grew a tail both sleek and long,
though it didn't really belong.
Although he tried every wizard's way
a rat he remains to this day.

He delved in books of every sort,
even pleaded in Wizard's Court.
They decided after much delay
that a rat he would have to stay.

And so we leave young Arthur Bell
with just this brief moral to tell;
if you meddle with things best left alone
you may spend years trying to atone.

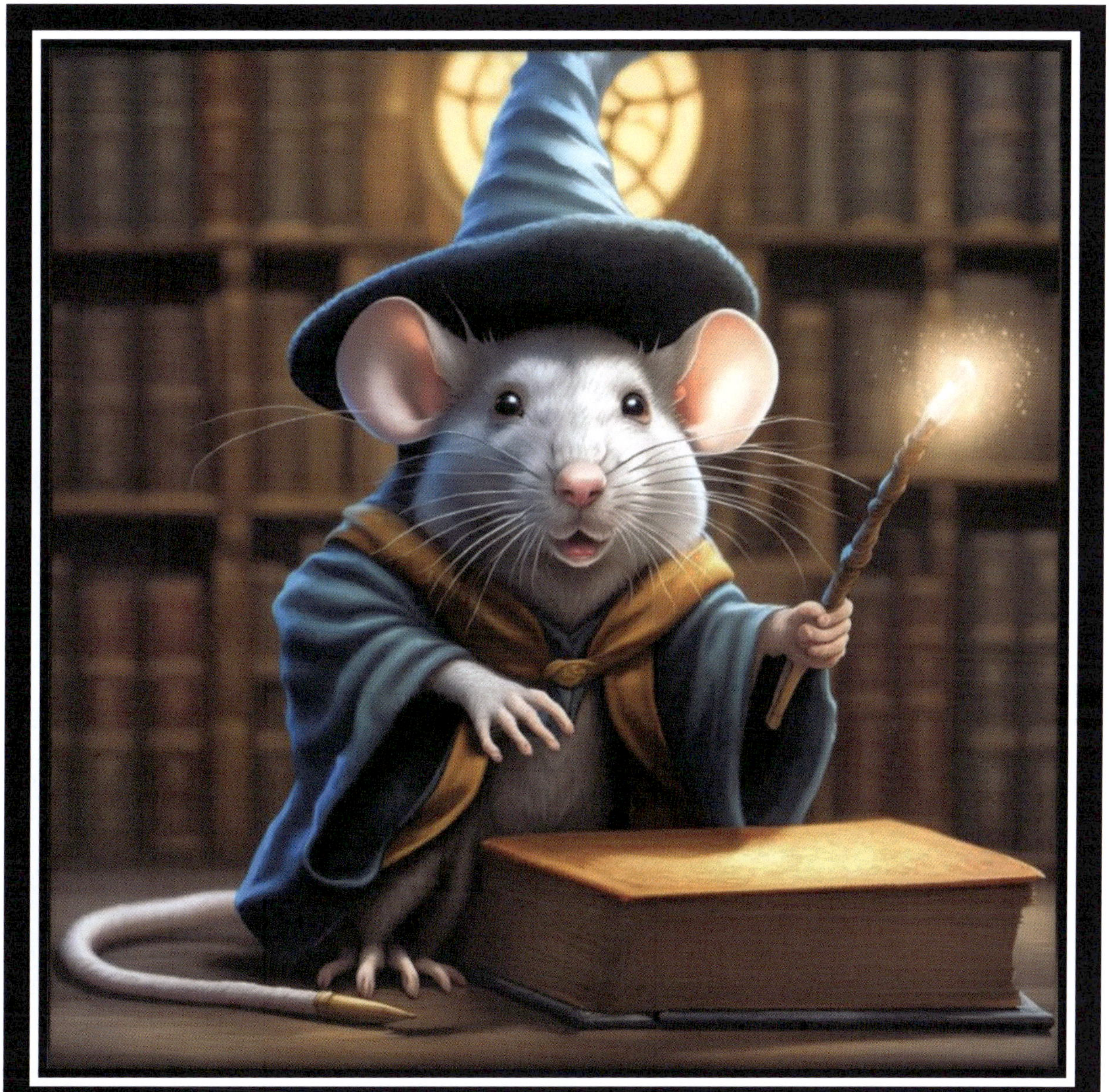

Slinky Rat

By Paula Montez

Now here's the tale of Slinky Rat
Who found a wizard's cosmic hat.
Enchantment oozed from brim to tip.
He snatched it in his scrawny grip.

Then mad with power, you know the type,
He conjured up a magic pipe,
Played it from the highest steeple
To rid the town of all its people.

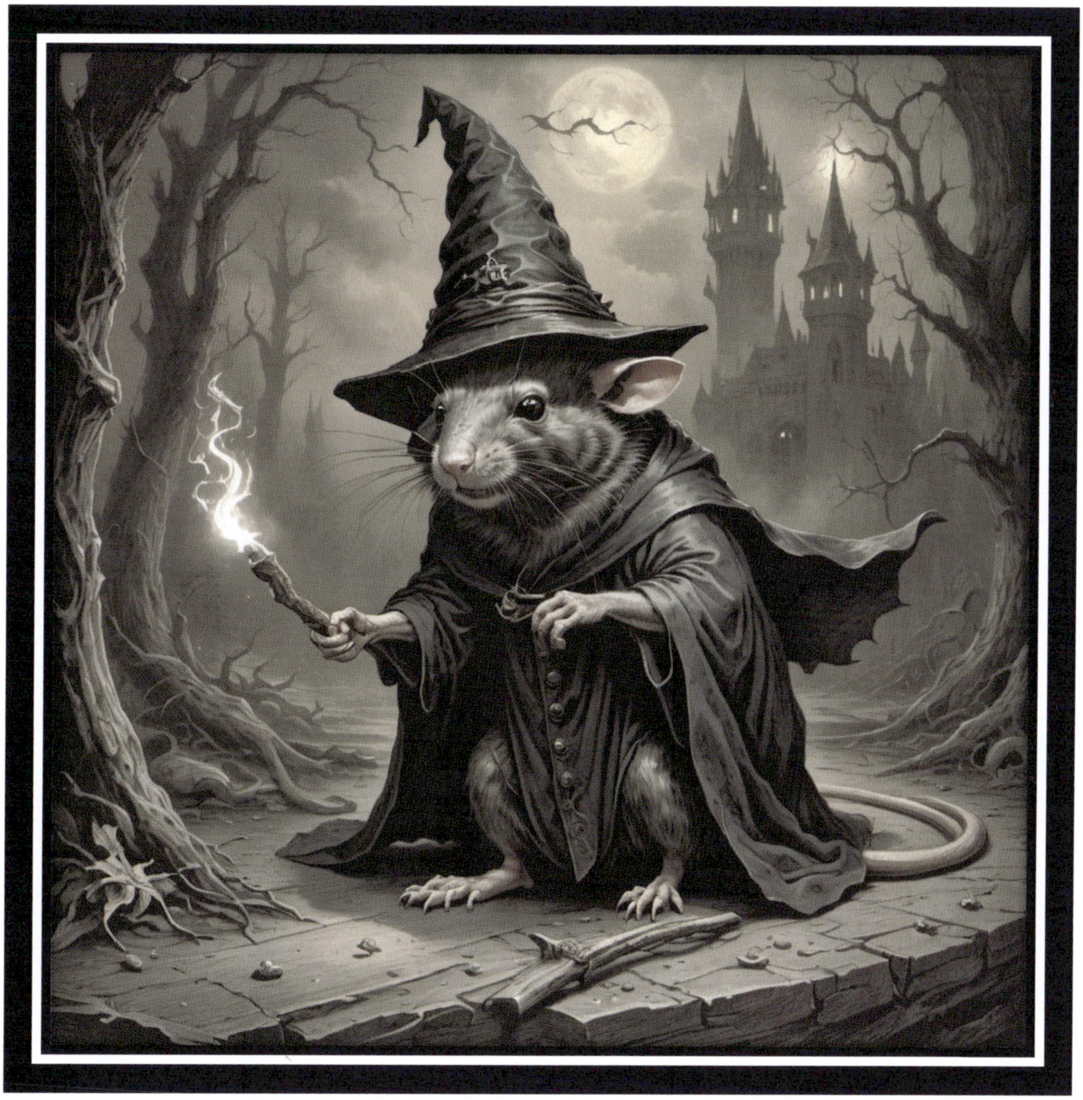

He led them out beneath the moon,

They danced, entranced by ancient tune.

Once free of humans as opponents

He planned to be the king of rodents.

He smirked and faced the hapless folk,

The music stopped - the spell then broke!

They screeched on seeing Slinky Rat,

Encircled him and squashed him flat.

The moral of this sorry story,

Is if you're seeking fame and glory

Don't toy with what you cannot master…..

And learn to make escape much faster.

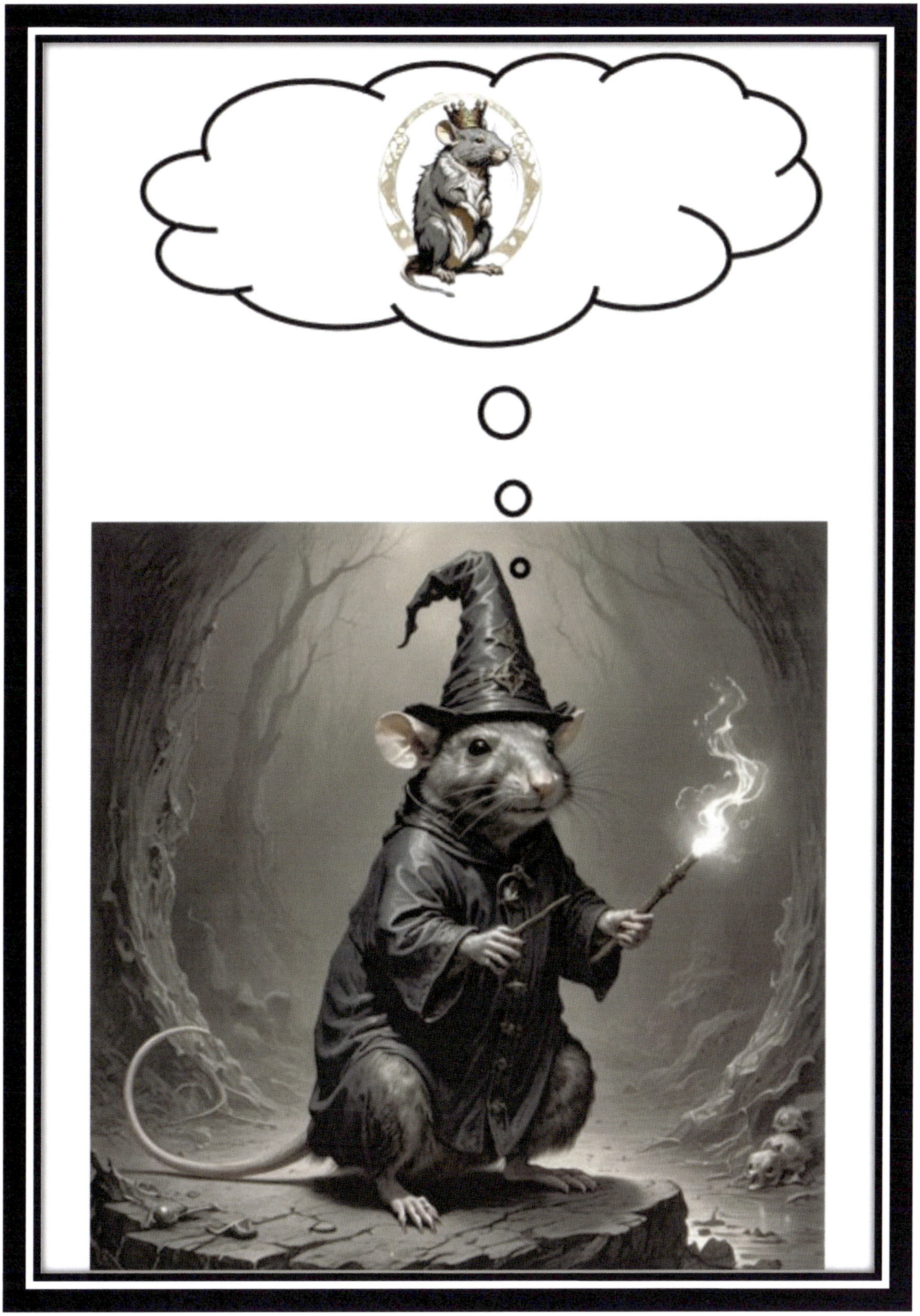

The Unemployed Wildfowling Dog

By Mark Lynch

Photos by Joe Olewnik

Featuring Mark Lynch and Molly

September the first is here.

I love this time of the year;

Splashing about on the estuarine marsh

Even when the weather`s most harsh.

Excited, tail wagging down by the shore,

Trouble is my Dad can`t hit a barn door.

I was hoping to retrieve some duck

But with his shooting no such luck.

Setting up ready, waiting for the flights,

Underneath his camo he`s wearing Mum's tights.

The excuses will come in thick and fast;

Won`t be the first won`t be the last

"I waited so long it threw off my timing",

Or the old "I had the wrong choke tube in"

The old classic: "the sun was in my eyes",

That one usually comes as no surprise

"The gun doesn`t fit without a heavy jacket"

So now he`s blaming it on the climate change racket.

"When you`re used to fast birds it`s hard to adjust."

Doubt he`d hit it if it was next to him eating a crust

"A victim of the unexpected"

"My swing got affected"

More excuses than the programme Billy Liar.

It`s a wonder his camo pants aren`t on fire.

Time you got quick on the draw

So I can put to use my paws.

A bang, but there`s nothing in the sea

Looks like it`s just chips for tea.

Acknowledgements

Thank you for reading!

And thanks to the authors for generously contributing their time and creativity to this project.

Ann-Marie	Joan	Brian	Fiona

Mark	Mike	Paula	Rhydderch

107

A bit about each author:

Ann Marie Thomas	Writing poetry and making up stories since she was a child, Ann Marie only began to write for publication when her children left home. She has since self published five medieval history books, a collection called Stories from Medieval Gower, and four science fiction novels, a series called Flight of the Kestrel. Following a major stroke she published a collection of poems written mostly in hospital, a surprisingly cheerful collection called 'My Stroke of Inspiration'.
Joan Darbyshire	Joan has been writing poetry since childhood and has had a few published in various magazines and anthologies

Brian Vincent	Whilst I have always done some writing, having a full-time job and a family with four children hampered my output and I was not able to take it more seriously until I retired. My main objective was short stories, but I dabbled in articles and poetry. My poems were mostly comic or of a narrative nature. The short stories were submitted to magazines and competitions with some successes which inspired me to continue to the present day.
Fiona Riley	Fiona enjoys writing poetry and short stories, mostly leaning towards the humorous although a few dark ones lurk in the background. Still trying to complete two novels after many years of procrastination, she lives in the hope that one day she will get around to them while she can still type, that they will be hugely successful and that they will facilitate her retirement! She should also mention that she is a dreamer.

Mark Lynch	I joined the SDWC two years ago after always wanting to write.. Subsequently I joined the poetry group of the SDWC which I`m enjoying immensely. Another ambition of mine was falconry which I`ve been active in for thirty years. This just leaves my remaining ambitions of being shot dead by a jealous husband at ninety-five years of age and having " Er, excuse me I ordered a pyramid" on my epitaph.
Mike Everley	Mike Everley has been writing for many years and has had poetry and short stories published in literary magazines. He was a member of both the NUJ and the Society of Authors before retirement.

Paula Montez	I have a selection of short poems on Instagram: @paula_montez_poetry. I have also published a book of longer poems called 'Views of the World' available on Amazon. More to follow in the future!
Rhydderch Wilson	Rhydderch is a horror author who writes under the name of Richard E. Rock (what he calls his 'immortal name'). His first novel DEEP LEVEL was published by Darkstroke Books in October 2020. His second, FRENZY ISLAND, was published by Cranthorpe Millner in October 2022.

Printed in Great Britain
by Amazon

d18c93e3-62de-491a-b776-ed8f78ca31f5R01